D0901715

Mary: God's Yes to Man

Mary:
God's Yes to Man

POPE JOHN PAUL II
Encyclical Letter
Mother of the Redeemer

Introduction by
Joseph Cardinal Ratzinger

Commentary by
Hans Urs von Balthasar

Ignatius Press   San Francisco

Title of the German original:
Maria: Gottes Ja zum Menschen
©1987 Verlag Herder
Freiburg im Breisgau

Cover design by Marcia Ryan

Cover art: *Madonna and Child*
by Franz Ittenbach
Used with kind permission
of Elena Wenzel

With ecclesiastical approval
©1988 Ignatius Press, San Francisco
ISBN 0–89870–219–4
Library of Congress catalogue number 88–80726
Printed in the United States of America

CONTENTS

The Sign of the Woman
by
Joseph Cardinal Ratzinger

Encyclical Letter
Mother of the Redeemer
by
Pope John Paul II

CONTENTS

Commentary
by
Hans Urs von Balthasar

The Sign of the Woman
An Introduction to the Encyclical "Redemptoris Mater"

by

CARDINAL JOSEPH RATZINGER

An encyclical on Mary, a Marian Year—neither exactly arouses enthusiasm among certain Catholics. They are concerned about negative interferences with the ecumenical dialogue. They see the danger of an overly emotional piety that will not measure up to serious theological standards. To be sure, the appearance of feminist thinking has added an unexpected new aspect that threatens to create some more confusion. On the one hand, feminists tell us that the Church's teaching on Mary simply codifies the dependency of women and glorifies their oppression. By extolling the Virgin and Mother, the obedient, humble servant, the role of women, as it were, has been restricted for centuries. Exalt the woman better to oppress her! On the other hand, however, the person of Mary is used by some to initiate a new and revolutionary interpretation of the Bible: liberation

This introduction, *The Sign of the Woman*, was translated from German by Rev. Lothar Krauth.

9

theology points to the "Magnificat", which proclaims that the mighty will be deposed, the lowly raised up. Thus Mary's song becomes the motto of a certain theology that considers it its duty to advocate the overthrow of established social structures.

A feminist reading of the Bible sees Mary as the emancipated woman who, uninhibited and conscious of her destiny, confronts a culture dominated by men. Together with other presumptive elements she is used as a "hermeneutical key" that allegedly discloses an original, totally different Christianity whose liberating energy was soon enough smothered and buried under the dominating male power structure. Such interpretations are easily recognized as tendentious and forced; but they still may do some good in directing our attention to the Bible and its uncorrupted message on Mary. This could well be the right moment, then, to expect more willing listeners for the teachings of a Marian encyclical whose entire purpose is to bring out what the Bible has to say.

In order to facilitate the reading and understanding of this papal document, I begin with some explanations about its specific methodology. A second section discusses four of its basic concepts.

I. METHODOLOGY

1. *Unity of the Bible*

The encyclical presents itself in large part as a meditation on the Bible. A historico-critical exegesis is presupposed; but the next step then leads to theological interpretation proper. What does this mean? How is it done? The basic rule for such an approach comes from Vatican II's Constitution on Divine Revelation, chapter 3:

> But, since Holy Scripture must be read and interpreted in the same spirit in which it was written, no less serious attention must be given to the content and unity of the whole of Scripture if the meaning of the sacred texts is to be correctly worked out. The living Tradition of the whole Church must be taken into account along with the harmony which exists between elements of the Faith (no. 12).

The basic precondition for all theological interpretation, therefore, lies in the conviction that Scripture is one book with a true inherent unity, in spite of its conflicting tensions, its many human authors, its long history of composition. This precondition, again, derives from the conviction that Scripture ultimately is the work of a single Author who appears under both a human and a divine aspect. First, Scripture originated with the one historical embodiment of the People of God who through all the turns of its history never lost its inner identity. Whenever this People of God is speaking, not just incidentally and on the surface but from the heart of its identity, it indeed speaks within the stages of its history, yet nevertheless always as one and the same subject. And this leads us to the second, the divine, aspect: this inner identity results from guidance by the one Spirit. Wherever the core of this identity is manifested, there speaks not merely a man or a people, but God himself in human words: the one Spirit who is the abiding inner power leading this People through its history.

Theological interpretation of Scripture, then, means this: not only to listen to the historical authors and their concurrent or conflicting messages, but also to search for the one voice in the totality of the texts, to search for the inner identity that sustains and unites this totality. A merely historical methodology, as it were, tries to single out specific facts neatly at the historical moment of their origins, thus isolating such a moment from all the rest and fixating it in its time. Theological interpretation, in contrast, while not disregarding this endeavor, goes further: the historical moment does not exist in isolation; indeed, it is part of a whole; it can be understood correctly only against the background and in the context of the whole. So, the methodology here is really very simple: Scripture interprets Scripture. Scripture interprets itself. Listening to Scripture's own interpretation through Scripture itself is a characteristic property of this encyclical. There is no attempt to explain the biblical texts in their individual moments through outside sources that may add much historical flavor, but no deeper understanding. Rather, the encyclical tries to let the biblical texts speak entirely on their own, in their multi-voiced diversity, and so it searches for an understanding from their inherent relationships.

Further, to emphasize the unity of Scripture implies a second principle: Scripture is to be read as a testimony for the present; it offers not just testimony about things and thoughts of the past but about timeless truth. This, too, cannot be the primary purpose of a strictly historical exegesis that looks back on Scripture's origin in the past and perforce reads it as a document of the past. From this, of course, we can learn something as well, as from all history, but only by analogy. The question about truth is essentially alien to modern science. It is a naive and unscientific question. And yet, it is the proper question of the Bible insofar as it is the Bible: What is truth? For enlightened Pilate this is a non-question; to pose it means already to dismiss it. We are not that different either. This question makes sense only if the Bible is a testimony for the present; if in the Bible we hear the words of someone who is present, and if this someone is distinguished from all other living subjects of history by being linked to the truth and so being able to proclaim truth in human language.

Faith in these principles lies at the core of all theological exegesis. With such an attitude, the Pope converses with the Bible. He considers the Bible's words within the larger biblical unity and accepts them as truth, as testimony about the true relationship between God and us. Thus the Bible is truly relevant for us; without any artificial up-dating it is in itself highly "up-to-date".

2. *The female line in the Bible*

The so-called Gospel of the Egyptians from the second century has Jesus say: "I have come to abolish the works of woman."[1] This expresses a basic theme in gnostic interpretations of the Christian message. It also appears, used somewhat differently, in the so-called Gospel of Thomas: "If you make the two into one . . . that which is above and that

[1] E. Hennecke and W. Schneemelcher, *Neutestamentliche Apokryphen*, I; *Evangelien* [New Testament Apocrypha, vol. I; the Gospels] (Tübingen, 1959), pp. 109–17; quotation p. 109. Cf. the related interesting comments in E. Kästner, *Die Stundentrommel vom heiligen Berg Athos* [The Hour-Drum from Sacred Mount Athos] (Frankfurt a.M., 1956), pp. 267ff.

which is below, and if you make into one what is male and what is female, so that what is male is no longer male, and what is female is no longer female . . . then you will enter the kingdom."[2] There we read further, in clear opposition to Galatians 4:4, "When you see the one who was not born of woman, fall on your face and worship. He is your Father."[3]

It is interesting, in this context, to note what Romano Guardini sees as an indication that in Saint John's writings the basic gnostic viewpoint has been overcome and rejected. He points out

[2] A. Guillaumont, H. C. Puech, G. Guispel, et al., "Logion 22", Coptic-German edition (Leiden, 1959). Parallels to logion 22 are found in several other logia, e.g., 37, 106, 46, 31 et al. Regarding the evaluation and dating of the Gospel of Thomas, cf. H. C. Puech, in Hennecke and Schneemelcher, *Neutestamentliche Apokryphen*, pp. 199–223. For very informative contributions to the interpretation of these texts cf. J. B. Bauer, "Echte Jesusworte?" [Truly Words of Jesus?], in W. C. van Unnik, *Evangelien aus dem Nilsand* [Gospels from the Sands of the Nile] (Frankfurt a.M., 1960), pp. 108–50. In view of the contemporary feminist discussion, it is important to be aware of the spiritual cultural background that underlies these texts; ancient Christianity took form against the confines of this background. This will help us recognize that Christianity in its organization and its determination of canonical writings safeguarded what was unique and new in Jesus' teaching, in opposition to prevailing attitudes that, dressed in religion, even claimed absolute status.

[3] A. Guillaumont, et al., "Logion 15".

that "the general architecture of the Book of Revelation accords men and women equal status, the way Christ intended it. True, in the figure of the Whore of Babylon the elements of being evil, lustful, and female do go together; but this would indicate a gnostic conception only if, on the other hand, all goodness were to reside exclusively in male figures. In truth, however, goodness finds a brilliant expression in the vision of the woman crowned with stars. If we still wanted to look for imbalance, then the female factor would seem rather favored; for the world, after its final redemption, appears as a bride."[4]

Guardini's observation clearly addresses a basic question regarding correct biblical interpretation. Gnostic exegesis is characterized by its identification of everything female with all that is mere matter, negative, worthless, and therefore not admissible into the salvific message of the Bible. Such a radical approach, of course, may provoke a totally opposite position, a revolt against its standards, turning them upside down.

[4] R. Guardini, *Das Christusbild der paulinischen und johanneischen Schriften* [The image of Christ in Saint Paul's and Saint John's Writings], 2nd ed. (Würzburg, 1961), p. 180. This study, somewhat overlooked, contains a wealth of important and until now neglected insights, not only regarding the basic aspects of theological exegesis but also regarding the correct understanding of Saint Paul's and Saint John's Christology as well.

In modern times, and for different reasons, there evolved a less radical, yet not less effective, elimination of everything female from the Bible's message. The overstated insistence on *Solus Christus!* (Christ alone!) logically led to the denial that we as creatures could cooperate with grace or respond to it on our own, which in this view would imply contempt for God's all-embracing grace. Consequently, nothing in the female line in the Bible, from Eve to Mary, could possibly have theological significance. All the respective pronouncements of the Church Fathers or medieval theologians were relentlessly branded as a reappearance of paganism, a betrayal of the one and only Savior. Contemporary radical feminism can probably only be understood as the final eruption of indignation about such extremes, promptly falling into the other extreme, indeed adopting truly pagan or neognostic positions. We witness here the rejection of the Father and the Son, a stab to the heart of the Bible's testimony.[5]

This makes it all the more important to read the Bible itself and read it in its entirety. Then it becomes evident that in the Old Testament, along-

[5] Indicative of the dissolving Christian concept of God in feminist thought is Carl F. X. Henry, *God, Revelation and Authority V* (Waco, Texas: Word Books, 1979). For an example of feminist interpretation of the New Testament cf. E. Schüssler-Fiorenza, *In Memory of Her: A Feminist Theological Reconstruction of Christian Origins* (New York, 1983).

side the line from Adam through the Patriarchs down to the Servant of God, there appears another line from Eve through the Matriarchs to figures like Deborah, Esther, Ruth and finally to the personified Divine Wisdom. This line simply cannot be dismissed theologically, although it is unfinished and its message openended, incomplete—just like the Old Testament as such, which still awaits the New Testament and its answer. The line from Adam receives its full meaning in Christ. Similarly, the significance of the female line in its inseparable interaction with the Christological mystery is revealed in Mary and in the symbolism applied to the Church. Major currents of contemporary theology ignore Mary and the Church, thus manifesting an inability to read the Bible in its totality. If we abandon the biblical concept of the Church, we lose the place where the unity of the Bible's testimony is experienced. This has inevitable logical consequences. On the other hand, in order to discern the Bible's complete fabric, we have to accept the Church as ground to stand on and thereby reject any historicist's pick-and-choose approach to the New Testament; an approach that attaches validity only to what is deemed more ancient and thus disparages Luke and John. Yet only by considering the whole do we comprehend the whole.[6]

[6] A tentative outline of these correlations is found in my

It seems to me that the actual importance of this encyclical stems not the least from its encouragement for us to rediscover the female line in the Bible with its specific significance in salvation history. We should become again aware that Christology does not exclude or suppress the female aspect as inconsequential, and that recognition of the female role does not diminish Christology. Only in the right coordination of one to the other can we discover the truth about God and ourselves. Those radical ideas of our time—which tear us apart and push class struggle to the very roots of human existence, namely, the relationship of man and woman—are heresies in the original meaning of the word: they pick and choose, and disregard the whole. We have to regain the whole of the biblical message in order to regain that spiritual center in which we as human beings become whole. The dramatic struggles of our time may well prompt a better appreciation of the call to read the Bible under a Marian perspective as well, a development which had seemed improbable only a short time ago. We need such a reading in order to deal with the anthropological challenge of our present era.

---

small volume, *Daughter Zion* (San Francisco: Ignatius Press, 1983).

3. *A historico-dynamic Mariology*

A linguistic observation may help us to understand better the specific Mariological reasoning of the encyclical. Mariological thought of the nineteenth and early twentieth centuries aimed foremost at the interpretation of Mary's privileges as summed up in her great honorary titles. After Mary's bodily Assumption into heaven was proclaimed as dogma, the dispute began to center on the title of "Mediatrix" and "Co-Redemptrix". The title "Co-Redemptrix", as far as I can discern, is not used at all in the encyclical. The title "Mediatrix" appears very seldom, mostly marginally and in quotations. The emphasis, instead, lies on the word "mediation", underlining its aspect of activity, of historical mission; the underlying reality transpires only through the mission, through historical action.[7]

This linguistic shift reveals the new approach to Mariology chosen by the Pope: not to display

[7] On the crisis of Mariology as related to the discussion prompted by the Council, cf. R. Laurentin, *La question mariale* [The Mariological question] (Paris, 1963); by the same author, *La vierge au Concile* [The Virgin and the Council] (Paris, 1965). A good synopsis of the present state of discussion is found in *Nuovo Dizionario di Mariologia* [New Dictionary of Mariology], ed. St. de Fiores and S. Meo (Editrice Paoline, 1985); cf. the articles "Mariologia/Marialogia" by de Fiores, pp. 891–920; "Mediatrice" by S. Meo, pp. 920–35.

before our wondering eyes any static, self-contained mysteries, but to enter into the dynamic quality of salvation that reaches out to us as a gift and a challenge and that assigns to us our place in history. Mary dwells not just in the past or in the lofty spheres of heaven under God's immediate disposition; she is and remains present and real in this historical moment; she is a person acting here and now. Her life is not just a reality that lies behind us, nor above us; she precedes us, as the Pope repeatedly emphasizes. She offers a key to interpret our present existence, not in theoretical discourse but in action, showing us the way that lies ahead. Within this framework, indeed, we also recognize who Mary *is*, who we *are*, yet only by considering the dynamic aspect of her role.

In the second part we shall have to consider in more detail how Mariology thus turns into a theology of history and a directive for action.

4. *Bimillenarianism?*

The Pope's first encyclical, *Redemptor Hominis*, already sounded a theme that returned with more emphasis in his encyclical of 1986 on the Holy Spirit, and that now occupies an important place in this Marian encyclical, namely, the anticipation of the year 2000, the great commemoration of Christ's birth "in the fullness of time" (Gal 4:4), which should be preceded by an Advent time of history and humanity. It may almost be safe to say that the two latter encyclicals intended to initiate such an Advent. The season of Advent, in the Church's liturgy, is the time of Mary: the time, indeed, when Mary offered her womb to receive the Savior of the world, when she carried in herself the expectations and hopes of all mankind. To celebrate Advent means to become like Mary, to enter into and become part of Mary's Yes, which, always anew, is the area of God's birth, of the "fullness of time".

The marked emphasis on the year 2000, and the interpretation of our present time from this view, cannot fail to provoke criticism. The question arises whether this might not be a new form of millenarianism, a numbers mysticism, which would miss the true importance of the Christ event. In its historical dimensions this event was unique and cannot be repeated; in its redemptive power it has been, ever since then, equally present to every moment; indeed, it bestows the aspect of eternity on all time. What we have said above already hints at the basic answer to these objections: the Risen Christ is in truth directly present to all time and so each moment is of equal value in relation to him. And yet, there do exist privileged occasions for remembrance: times of celebration. John Paul II, in a short discourse on famous Marian shrines, points out that in spite of

God's presence everywhere, and in spite of Christ's sacramental presence in every tabernacle around the world, we still find a certain "geography of faith". Similarly, there are certain structures of time that invite us to reflect, to recognize God's revelation in our human time and thus to experience God's perpetual presence to us.

Raniero Cantalamessa, in this context, points to a helpful observation that Saint Augustine develops in his theology of celebration. The great Doctor says in one of his letters that there are two kinds of celebrations: those which simply observe an annual commemoration, the recurrence of a specific date; and those which celebrate holy mysteries. The former emphasize a specific date to awaken remembrance; the latter do not center on a particular date as such but rather on entering into the inner reality of some outward event and identifying with this reality.[8]

We can say, then, that the jubilee of the year 2000 does not so much celebrate a particular date —and not at all as if such a date itself would automatically accomplish anything—the way a

[8] R. Cantalamessa, "Maria e lo Spirito Santo" [Mary and the Holy Spirit], in *Verso il terzo millenio sotto l'azione dello Spirito. Per una Lettura della "Dominum et Vivificantem"* [Approaching the Third Millennium of the Spirit's action. Commentary on "Dominum et Vivificantem"], H.U. von Balthasar et al. (Editrice Vaticana, 1986), pp. 49–55. Saint Augustine, *Ep. 55*, 1.2 *CSEL* 34, I, p. 170.

clock strikes at the present time. Decisive, rather, is the reminder inherent in our chronology as such and identified again by any jubilee: that God holds all time in his hands. He is the "Holy Mystery", both touching and transcending time; and so he enables us, in this ever-changing, ever-flowing stream of time, to find firm ground to stand on, to grasp the abiding elements in all that passes away.

II. FOUR BASIC CONCEPTS

1. *Mary, woman of faith*

The central attitude by which Mary is defined in the encyclical is faith. Jesus is the Incarnate Word; he speaks from the depth of his union with the Father.[9] Mary's nature, however, and her life are essentially determined by her faith. "Blessed is she who believed" (Lk 1:45); this acclamation by Elizabeth addressed to Mary becomes the key concept in Mariology. Mary thus joins the circle

[9] On Christ's knowledge and self-awareness cf. the illuminating document by the International Theological Commission, *De Jesu autoconscientia quam scilicet de se ipso et de sua missione habuit* [Jesus' Awareness Regarding Himself and His Mission], Latin and Italian ed. (Editrice Vaticana, 1986). Helpful also F. Dreyfus, *Jésus savait-il qu'il était Dieu?* [Was Jesus Aware of His Divinity?] (Paris, 1984).

of great men of faith, who are praised in the Letter to the Hebrews (chapter 11) whereby all
commemoration of faith-heroes is given its theological place. This fundamental biblical ground
is sustained throughout the encyclical and should
always be remembered for a correct understanding.
Thus the encyclical turns into a catechesis about
faith as well as about the basic relationship of man
to God. The Pope sees Mary's attitude in relation
to Abraham: just as Abraham's faith stands at the
beginning of the Old Covenant, so Mary's faith at
the Annunciation opens the New Covenant. Mary's
faith, like Abraham's, means trust in God and
obedience, even when one walks in darkness. It
means letting go of oneself, freeing oneself, sur-
rendering oneself in view of the truth, of God.
Hence faith, in the obscurity of God's inscrutable
ways, becomes conformity with him (*RM*, no. 14).

The Pope sees Mary's Yes, her act of faith,
interpreted as well in that Psalm passage which the
Letter to the Hebrews understands as the Son's
Yes to the Incarnation and the Cross: "Sacrifice
and offering you did not desire, but a body you
have prepared for me . . . I have come to do your
will, O God" (Heb 10:5–7; Ps 40:6–8; *RM*, no.
13). In her Yes to the birth of God's Son from her
own womb, through the power of the Holy Spirit,
Mary makes her body, her very self, into the place
of God's presence. In this Yes, therefore, Mary's

will and the Son's will coincide. Through the one
accord of "Yes", "A body you have prepared for
me", the Incarnation becomes possible; and Mary,
as Saint Augustine remarks, conceived in her spirit
before conceiving in her body.[10]

Faith includes suffering, as Abraham had to
learn thoroughly, and as Mary experienced first in
the encounter with Simeon, and then again in the
loss and finding of the boy Jesus. The Pope clearly
wishes to stress the words of the Gospel: "But
they did not grasp what he said to them" (Lk
2:48–50; *RM*, no. 17). Even in intimate closeness
to Jesus, the mystery remains mystery, and Mary
cannot approach it but in faith. Yet just in this way
she remains truly in touch with the new self-
revelation of God, which is Incarnation. Indeed,
because she is one of the "lowly ones" who accept
the measure of faith, she stands in the promise:
"Father . . . , what you have hidden from the
learned and the clever you have revealed to the
merest children. . . . No one knows the Son but
the Father" (Mt 11:25–27; *RM*, no. 17).

The meditation on Mary's faith finds its culmination and summation in the interpretation of

[10] The Pope, in his encyclical (*RM*, no. 13), draws on
several Augustinian texts which underline the teaching "prius
mente quam ventre" [first in spirit, then in body], e.g., *De
sancta virginitate* [On virginity] III, 3, *PL* 40, p. 398; "Sermon
215", 4 *PL* 38, p. 1074.

Mary's standing under the Cross. As the woman of faith she diligently "treasures in her heart" all the words she has received (Lk 1:29; 2:19, 51). But under the Cross the great promise given to her, "The Lord God will give him the throne of David his father . . . and his kingdom will have no end" (Lk 1:32–35), appears definitely false. Here, faith has reached its utmost humiliation (*kenosis*), stands in total darkness. Yet just then is it fully united with the utmost humiliation (*kenosis*) of Jesus (Phil 2:5–8). Things here have come full circle: "A body you have prepared for me. . . . Lo, I have come to do your will." Now this offer of self-surrender has been accepted, and Mary's faith in darkness is precisely the culmination of that unity of will discussed at the beginning of this reflection. Faith —evident since Abraham—means communion with the Cross, and only on the Cross does faith find its highest fulfillment. In this and no other way will faith merit God's "Blessed are you." "You have revealed it to the merest children."

2. *The Sign of the Woman*

The catechesis on faith implies the notion of a process and therefore of history. Hence it is not surprising that in a second train of thought, the encyclical, always closely following the biblical text, points to Mary as a guide in history, as a sign of the times. The twelfth chapter of Revelation presents the Sign of the Woman, a sign appearing at a certain moment in history in order to determine from then on the interrelation of heaven and earth. This passage distinctly recalls to the biblical account of the beginning of history, those mysterious lines traditionally called the *proto-evangelium* (first Gospel): "I will put enmity between you and the woman and between your offspring and hers; he will strike at your head, while you strike at his heel" (Gen 3:15).

The Church Fathers took this judgment on the serpent after the Fall as the first promise of a Redeemer, a reference to the offspring who will smash the serpent's head. History, then, was never without "gospel", without the Good News. The instant of the Fall became the beginning of the promise. The Fathers considered it important, too, that right at this first beginning we find the Christological and Mariological themes intimately intertwined. This primeval promise, obscure as it is, and deciphered only in the light of later texts, is a promise given to the woman, to come about through the woman.

The analysis of this text makes it clear that all revelation is a process, yielding its full message only as a whole. The meaning of the ensuing history unfolds in three actors: the woman, the offspring, the serpent. The offspring promises blessing and liberation: he strikes at the serpent's head. But the curse, the bondage, retain their power: the serpent strikes at his heel. Blessing and curse may remain in balance, the outcome is uncertain. In the Book of Revelation all three actors return. The drama of history has reached its climax. The outcome, however, has already been determined by the event at Nazareth. "Hail, full of grace", the angel had greeted Mary who now reappears as the woman whose blessing is complete.

Following his principle of interpreting Scripture with Scripture, the Pope sheds light on this blessing formula by relating it to the opening of the Letter to the Ephesians. There we find identical expressions and thus a key to unlock that blessing's fuller meaning: "Praised be the God and Father of our Lord Jesus Christ, who has bestowed on us in Christ every spiritual blessing in the heavens! God chose us in him before the world began . . . he likewise predestined us through Jesus Christ to be his adopted sons . . . that all might praise the glorious grace he has bestowed on us" (Eph 1:3–6; *RM*, nos. 7–11). The expression "full of grace" points to that fullness of blessing mentioned in Paul's Letter. The Letter further implies that "the Son", once and for all, has directed the drama of history toward the blessing. Mary, therefore, who gave birth to him, is truly "full of grace"—she becomes a sign in history. The angel greeted Mary, and from then on it is clear that the blessing is stronger than the curse. The sign of the woman has become the sign of hope, leading the way to hope. The sign of the woman reveals God's favor toward humanity, a favor "more powerful than all manifestation of evil and sin, all that 'enmity' that constantly has shaped the course of human history" (*RM*, no. 11).

Seen from this viewpoint, the Marian Year expresses the Pope's desire, in this our era, to hold up the "Sign of the Woman" as the essential "sign of the times". On the path traced by this sign we journey in hope toward Christ, who through this guiding light directs the paths of history.

3. *Mary's role of mediation*

Another theme I wish to single out is the teaching on Mary's role of mediation, dealt with extensively in the Pope's encyclical. This topic, without doubt, will attract most of the theological and ecumenical discussion. It is true, the Second Vatican Council has already mentioned the title "Mediatrix"[11] and spoken about Mary's mediation;[12] yet this theme, so far, has not been thoroughly developed in the Magisterium's documents. Regarding the subject

[11] *Lumen Gentium*, no. 62.
[12] Ibid., nos. 60 and 62.

itself, the encyclical does not extend the Council's teaching whose terminology it follows. But the encyclical deepens the Council's premises and thus gives them more substance for study and devotion.

First, let me briefly clarify the terms with which the Pope defines theologically the notion of mediation and guards it against misunderstandings; only then can the positive intention be adequately understood. The Holy Father strongly emphasizes Jesus Christ as the sole mediator. But this mediation is not exclusive, rather inclusive, allowing forms of participation. In other words, Christ as the only mediator does not take away our task to stand before God as persons linked to each other and responsible for each other. We all, in different ways and in union with Jesus Christ, can be mediators for each other in our approach to God. This is a simple matter of fact, evident in daily experiences; for nobody stands in the Faith all alone, everybody depends for a living faith on human mediation. No such human mediation, though, would suffice to build the bridge to God; human beings, by themselves, can never offer absolute assurance of God's existence and his presence. Yet in union with the One who himself is this presence, we can and do act as mediators for each other.

With this, the general possibility and outline of

mediation in relation to Christ is defined. The
Pope develops his terminology from there. Mary's
mediation is based on participation in Christ's
mediation; compared to his role, hers is one of
subordination. These terms are taken from the
Council's texts, as is the further statement: this
role "flows forth from the superabundance of the
merits of Christ, rests on his mediation, depends
entirely on it and draws all its power from it"
(*RM*, no. 22; *Lumen Gentium*, no. 60). Mary's
mediation, therefore, is accomplished in intercession (*RM*, no. 21).

Everything said so far applies to Mary as well as
to any human participation in Christ's mediating
role. In all of this, Mary's mediation is not different from any other comparable human mediation. But the Pope does not leave it at that. Even
though Mary's mediation happens on the same
level as our common human participation in the
Savior's mission, hers is nevertheless above the
"ordinary". It uniquely surpasses the mediating
role that all of us, as members in the communion
of saints, are empowered to exercise. The encyclical, again, develops these thoughts with constant reference to the biblical text.

An initial aspect of Mary's unique mediating
role is identified by the Pope in a profound reflection on the miracle at Cana. There, Mary's
intercession prompts Jesus to anticipate in a sign

his coming "hour"—as it happens again and again in the "signs" of the Church, the sacraments. The conceptual definition proper of Mary's special role of mediation occurs in part three of the encyclical, again by subtly connecting diverse Scripture passages that seemingly are unrelated, and yet, when considered together—remember the unity of the Bible!—yield surprising insights. The Pope's basic thesis is this: Mary's mediation is unique because it is maternal mediation, related to Christ who is always born anew into this world. Her mediation thus represents the female dimension in salvation history; this female dimension is forever centered in Mary's role. Of course, if the Church is conceived only as an institution, only as the result of majority decisions and managed activities, then there is no room for such reflections. The Pope, in contrast to a readily accepted sociological notion of the Church, reminds us of a Pauline statement that has not received its due consideration: "You are my children, and you put me back in labor pains until Christ is formed in you" (Gal 4:19). Life is not "made" but born, and not without labor pains. The "motherly awareness of the early Church", identified here by the Pope, has great significance for our own time (RM, no. 43).

Now, we could indeed ask the question, Why do we have to think that this female and motherly dimension of the Church is residing forever in

Mary? The encyclical's answer begins with a
Scripture passage, which at first sight seems to
discourage any Marian devotion. When the unknown woman, excited after hearing Jesus, breaks
out in praise of the "womb that bore" such a man,
the Lord retorts, "Rather, blest are they who hear
the word of God and keep it" (Lk 11:28). The
Holy Father connects this text with the Lord's
similar saying: "My mother and my brothers are
those who hear the word of God and act upon it"
(Lk 8:20f.).

It seems as if these were anti-Marian statements.
In truth, however, these passages reveal two important insights. First, beyond the unique physical
birth of Christ, there exists another dimension of
motherhood, which is and must be more comprehensive. And secondly, this motherhood, which
constantly gives birth to Jesus, is founded on the
hearing, keeping, and doing of his word.

It is again Luke, whose Gospel provided these
two passages, who depicts Mary as the exemplary
hearer of the Word; for she carries the Word within
her, preserves it, and nurtures it to completion.
This means that Luke, by handing on the Lord's
two quoted sayings, does not really contradict any
Marian devotion but rather wants to anchor it in
its true foundation. He shows that Mary's motherhood is not just based on the biological event,
which happened once, but on the fact that in her

total being, Mary was, and is, and therefore will remain, a mother. Pentecost, the birth of the Church by the Holy Spirit, shows this in factual terms: Mary is in the midst of the praying assembly that, by the Spirit's Advent, becomes Church. The analogy between Christ's Incarnation by the power of the Spirit at Nazareth, and the birth of the Church on Pentecost, cannot be disregarded. "The person who links these two moments is Mary" (*RM*, no. 24). The Pope wishes to propose the scene of Pentecost as the unique sacred symbol of our time, the symbol of the Marian Year, the sign of hope for this our era (*RM*, no. 33).

What Luke brings out in a texture of interrelated hints, the Pope finds fully developed in Saint John's Gospel, in the words of the Crucified to his Mother and to John, the beloved disciple. The words, "There is your mother", and "Woman, there is your son", have at all times inspired the exegetes to reflect on the special role of Mary in and for the Church; any Marian reflection rightly centers on these words. The Holy Father takes them to be the crucified Christ's last will and testament. Here, at the very center of the paschal mystery, Mary is given as mother to all humanity. Mary's motherhood receives a new dimension, the consequence of her untainted love come to perfection at the foot of the Cross (*RM*, no. 23).

The "Marian dimension in the life of Christ's disciples . . . not only of John, but of every disciple, every Christian" is thus manifested. "Mary's motherhood, our legacy, is a gift that Christ himself bestows on each one of us" (*RM*, no. 45).

The Holy Father offers here a subtle analysis of the passage that concludes this scene in the Gospel, customarily translated as, "From that hour onward, the disciple took her into his care" (Jn 19:27). The full depth, however, of what is happening here, so the Pope emphasizes, is revealed only in a strictly literal translation. Then, in fact, we read: he took her into his own. This, for the Holy Father, means a special personal relationship between the disciple—any disciple—and Mary, the admission of Mary into the innermost regions of one's mental and spiritual life, the entry into her reality as woman and mother. All this becomes a way to bring forth Christ always anew, and leads a disciple to conform to the image of Christ. Thus the Marian challenge defines the role of womanhood, the feminine dimension of the Church, and the specific vocation of women in the Church (*RM*, no. 46).

All the Scripture passages converge, once their correlation within one fabric of thought has been shown in the encyclical. For the Gospel writer John, in the Cana passage as well as the crucifixion account, does not use Mary's proper name, nor the title "Mother", but "Woman". The correlation to chapter three of Genesis and chapter twelve of Revelation, to the "Sign of the Woman", is thus suggested by these texts. Without doubt, John's specific expressions are designed to show Mary simply as "the woman", a figure of general and symbolic significance.[13] The crucifixion account, then, turns into an interpretation of history, pointing to the "Sign of the Woman", to her who with maternal care takes part in the struggle against the powers of negation and so becomes our sign of hope (*RM*, nos. 24 and 47). Everything that follows from these texts is summed up in the encyclical in a statement from Pope Paul's Profession of Faith: "We believe that the most holy Mother of God, the new Eve, the Mother of the Church, carries on in heaven her maternal role with regard to the members of Christ, cooperating in the birth and development of divine life in the souls of the redeemed" (*RM*, no. 47).

[13] Regarding the contemporary debate on Jn 19:26f. cf. R. Schnackenburg, *Das Johannesevangelium* III, 5th ed. [Saint John's Gospel] (Freiburg im Breisgau, 1986), pp. 321–28; R. E. Brown, K. P. Donfried, J. A. Fitzmyer, J. Reumann, *Mary in the New Testament* (Philadelphia and New York, 1978), pp. 206–18; N. M. Flanagan, "Mary in the Theology of John's Gospel" (March 4, 1978), pp. 110–20.

4. *Meaning of the Marian Year*

Using all these elements, the Pope finally constructs the meaning of the new Marian Year. While the Marian Year of Pius XII was connected with the two dogmas of the Immaculate Conception and the Assumption, this Marian Year centers on the special presence of the Blessed Mother within the mystery of Christ and his Church (*RM*, no. 48). The purpose of this new Marian Year is not only to remind, but to prepare (*RM*, no. 49); its dynamic aspect points toward the future. The Pope recalls the Millennium of the baptism of Saint Vladimir, an event which may also be considered the Millennium of Russia's conversion to Christianity, and relates this to the bi-Millennium of Christ's birth. Such dates demand not only remembrance, but much more a renewed awareness of our true historical and human identity transpiring in these dates. Such renewed orientation of our history toward its foundations is the profoundest meaning of this Jubilee Year. At this historical moment, with its explosion of new knowledge combined with a crisis of all spiritual values, who would deny our dire need for the repositioning of our existence?

The time frame chosen by the Pope for the Marian Year strikingly underlines its inner meaning. It begins with Pentecost. The scene of Pentecost, as mentioned above, should become the sacred symbol of our identity and so of our true hope. The Church has to learn anew from Mary how to be "authentic Church". Only through a re-orientation toward the Sign of the Woman, toward the correctly defined female dimension of the Church, will come about the new openness for the Spirit's creative power and our transformation into the image and likeness of Christ, whose presence alone can give direction and hope to history. The Marian Year closes with the Feast of Mary's bodily Assumption into heaven, and thus directs our gaze toward the great sign of hope, toward humanity's final salvation anticipated in Mary, in whom is revealed the realm where salvation, indeed all salvation, is accomplished.

The Pope uses the conclusion of the encyclical to identify in striking, practical terms the coordinates of our time and thus the purpose of the Marian Year. We already mentioned that he sees our era as a new time of Advent. In this context, he now interprets the ancient Advent hymn "Alma Redemptoris Mater" and emphasizes its line, "Assist your people who have fallen yet strive to rise again." The Marian Year, as it were, is situated at the critical line between falling and rising, in the twilight between the striking at the serpent's head, and the striking at man's vulnerable heel. We find ourselves in this situation still, and always anew.

The Marian Year intends to challenge everyone's conscience to choose the path of non-falling, to learn from Mary about this path. In a sense, it is intended to be one loud cry for help, "Assist, oh, assist your people who are falling!" (*RM*, no. 52). In the conception of the encyclical, the Marian Year stands far from mere sentimental devotion. It implores our generation to recognize the call of this historical hour, and to direct our steps onto the path that protects from falling, even in the midst of countless dangers.

Encyclical Letter
Mother of the Redeemer
On the Blessed Virgin Mary
In the Life of the Pilgrim Church

by

POPE JOHN PAUL II

Venerable Brothers,
Beloved Sons and Daughters,
Health and the Apostolic Blessing!

INTRODUCTION

1. The Mother of the Redeemer has a precise place in the plan of salvation, for "when the time had fully come, God sent forth his Son, born of woman, born under the law, to redeem those who were under the law, so that we might receive adoption as sons. And because you are sons, God has sent the Spirit of his Son into our hearts, crying 'Abba! Father!' " (Gal 4:4–6).

With these words of the Apostle Paul, which the Second Vatican Council takes up at the beginning of its treatment of the Blessed Virgin Mary,[1] I too wish to begin my reflection on the role of Mary in the mystery of Christ and on her active

The English edition of *Redemptoris Mater* was originally published in *L'Osservatore Romano*, March 30, 1987.

[1] Cf. Second Vatican Ecumenical Council, Dogmatic Constitution on the Church *Lumen Gentium*, 52 and the whole of Chapter VIII, entitled "The Role of the Blessed Virgin Mary, Mother of God, in the Mystery of Christ and the Church".

and exemplary presence in the life of the Church. For they are words which celebrate together the love of the Father, the mission of the Son, the gift of the Spirit, the role of the woman from whom the Redeemer was born, and our own divine filiation, in the mystery of the "fullness of time".[2]

This "fullness" indicates the moment fixed from all eternity when the Father sent his Son, "that whoever believes in him should not perish but have eternal life" (Jn 3:16). It denotes the blessed moment when the Word that "was with God . . . became flesh and dwelt among us" (Jn 1:1, 14), and made himself our brother. It marks the moment when the Holy Spirit, who had already in-

[2] The expression "fullness of time" (πλήρωμα τοῦ χρόνου) is parallel with similar expressions of Judaism both Biblical (cf. Gen 29:21; 1 Sam 7:12; Tob 14:5) and extra-Biblical, and especially in the New Testament (cf. Mk 1:15; Lk 21:24; Jn 7:8; Eph 1:10). From the point of view of form, it means not only the conclusion of a chronological process but also and especially the coming to maturity or completion of a particularly important period, one directed toward the fulfillment of an expectation, a coming to completion which thus takes on an eschatological dimension. According to Gal 4:4 and its context, it is the coming of the Son of God that reveals that time has, so to speak, reached its limit. That is to say, the period marked by the promise made to Abraham and by the Law mediated by Moses has now reached its climax, in the sense that Christ fulfills the divine promise and supersedes the old law.

fused the fullness of grace into Mary of Nazareth,
formed in her virginal womb the human nature of
Christ. This "fullness" marks the moment when,
with the entrance of the eternal into time, time
itself is redeemed, and being filled with the mystery
of Christ becomes definitively "salvation time".
Finally, this "fullness" designates the hidden beginning of the Church's journey. In the liturgy the
Church salutes Mary of Nazareth as the Church's
own beginning,[3] for in the event of the Immaculate
Conception the Church sees projected, and anticipated in her most noble member, the saving grace
of Easter. And above all, in the Incarnation she
encounters Christ and Mary indissolubly joined:
he who is the Church's Lord and Head and she
who, uttering the first *fiat* of the New Covenant,
prefigures the Church's condition as spouse and
mother.

2. Strengthened by the presence of Christ (cf. Mt
28:20), the Church journeys through time toward
the consummation of the ages and goes to meet
the Lord who comes. But on this journey—and I
wish to make this point straightaway—she pro-
ceeds along the path already trodden by the Virgin

[3] Cf. Roman Missal, Preface of December 8th, Immaculate
Conception of the Blessed Virgin Mary; Saint Ambrose, *De
Institutione Virginis*, XV, 93–94: *PL* 16, 342; *Lumen Gentium*, 68.

Mary, who *"advanced in her pilgrimage of faith, and loyally persevered in her union with her Son unto the Cross"*.[4]

I take these very rich and evocative words from the Constitution *Lumen Gentium*, which in its concluding part offers a clear summary of the Church's doctrine on the Mother of Christ, whom she venerates as her beloved Mother and as her model in faith, hope, and charity.

Shortly after the Council, my great predecessor Paul VI decided to speak further of the Blessed Virgin. In the Encyclical *Christi Matri* and subsequently in the Apostolic Exhortations *Signum Magnum* and *Marialis Cultus*[5] he expounded the foundations and criteria of the special veneration which the Mother of Christ receives in the Church, as well as the various forms of Marian devotion—liturgical, popular, and private—which respond to the spirit of faith.

3. The circumstance which now moves me to take up this subject once more is *the prospect of the year 2000*, now drawing near, in which the Bi-

[4] *Lumen Gentium*, 58.

[5] Pope Paul VI, Encyclical Letter *Christi Matri* (September 15, 1966): *AAS* 58 (1966) 745–49; Apostolic Exhortation *Signum Magnum* (May 13, 1967): *AAS* 59 (1967) 465–75; Apostolic Exhortation *Marialis Cultus* (February 2, 1974): *AAS* 66 (1974) 113–68.

millennial Jubilee of the birth of Jesus Christ at the same time directs our gaze toward his Mother. In recent years, various opinions have been voiced suggesting that it would be fitting to precede that anniversary by a similar Jubilee in celebration of the birth of Mary.

In fact, even though it is not possible to establish an exact *chronological point* for identifying the date of Mary's birth, the Church has constantly been aware that *Mary appeared* on the horizon of *salvation history before Christ*.[6] It is a fact that when "the fullness of time" was definitively drawing near— the saving advent of Emmanuel—she who was from all eternity destined to be his Mother already existed on earth. The fact that she "preceded" the coming of Christ is reflected every year *in the liturgy of Advent*. Therefore, if to that ancient historical expectation of the Savior we compare these years which are bringing us closer to the end of the second Millennium after Christ and to the beginning of the third, it becomes fully comprehensible that in this present period we wish to turn in a special way to her, the one who in the "night" of the Advent expectation began to shine like a true "Morning Star" (*Stella Matutina*). For just as this star, together with the "dawn", precedes the

[6] The Old Testament foretold in many different ways the mystery of Mary: cf. Saint John Damascene, *Hom. in Dormitionem* I, 8–9: S. Ch. 80, 103–107.

rising of the sun, so Mary from the time of her
Immaculate Conception preceded the coming of
the Savior, the rising of the "Sun of Justice" in the
history of the human race.[7]

Her presence in the midst of Israel—a presence
so discreet as to pass almost unnoticed by the eyes
of her contemporaries—shone very clearly before
the Eternal One, who had associated this hidden
"daughter of Zion" (cf. Zeph 3:14; Zech 2:10)
with the plan of salvation embracing the whole
history of humanity. With good reason then at the
end of this Millennium, we Christians who know
that the providential plan of the Most Holy Trinity
is *the central reality of Revelation and of faith* feel the
need to emphasize the unique presence of the
Mother of Christ in history, especially during
these last years leading up to the year 2000.

4. The Second Vatican Council prepares us for
this by presenting in its teaching *the Mother of God
in the mystery of Christ and of the Church*. If it is true,
as the Council itself proclaims,[8] that "only in the
mystery of the Incarnate Word does the mystery

[7] Cf. *Insegnamenti di Giovanni Paolo II*, VI/2 (1983) 225f.;
Pope Pius IX, Apostolic Letter *Ineffabilis Deus* (December 8,
1854): *Pii IX P.M. Acta*, pars I, 597–99.

[8] Cf. Second Vatican Ecumenical Council, Pastoral Constitution on the Church in the Modern World *Gaudium et
Spes*, 22.

of man take on light" then this principle must be
applied in a very particular way to that exceptional
"daughter of the human race", that extraordinary
"woman" who became the Mother of Christ.
Only *in the mystery of Christ is her mystery fully made
clear*. Thus has the Church sought to interpret it
from the very beginning: the mystery of the Incarnation has enabled her to penetrate and to make
ever clearer the mystery of the Mother of the
Incarnate Word. The Council of Ephesus (431)
was of decisive importance in clarifying this, for
during that Council, to the great joy of Christians,
the truth of the divine motherhood of Mary was
solemnly confirmed as a truth of the Church's
faith. Mary *is the Mother of God (= Theotókos)*,
since by the power of the Holy Spirit she conceived
in her virginal womb and brought into the world
Jesus Christ, the Son of God who is of one being
with the Father.[9] "The Son of God . . . born of
the Virgin Mary . . . has truly been made one of
us",[10] has been made man. Thus, through the
mystery of Christ, on the horizon of the Church's
faith there shines in its fullness the mystery of his
Mother. In turn, the dogma of the divine motherhood of Mary was for the Council of Ephesus and

[9] Ecumenical Council of Ephesus, in *Conciliorum Oecumenicorum Decreta*, Bologna 1973, 41–44, 59–61: *DS* 250–64;
cf. Ecumenical Council of Chalcedon, o.c. 84–87:*DS* 300–303.

[10] *Gaudium et Spes*, 22.

is for the Church like a seal upon the dogma of the Incarnation, in which the Word truly assumes human nature into the unity of his person, without canceling out that nature.

5. The Second Vatican Council, by presenting Mary in the mystery of Christ, also finds the path to a deeper understanding of the mystery of the Church. Mary, as the Mother of Christ, *is in a particular way united with the Church*, "which the Lord established as his own body".[11] It is significant that the conciliar text places this truth about the Church as the Body of Christ (according to the teaching of the Pauline Letters) in close proximity to the truth that the Son of God "through the power of the Holy Spirit was born of the Virgin Mary". The reality of the Incarnation finds a sort of extension *in the mystery of the Church—the Body of Christ*. And one cannot think of the reality of the Incarnation without referring to Mary, the Mother of the Incarnate Word.

In these reflections, however, I wish to consider primarily that "pilgrimage of faith" in which "the Blessed Virgin advanced", faithfully preserving her union with Christ.[12] In this way the "*twofold bond*" which unites the Mother of God *with Christ and with the Church* takes on historical significance.

[11] *Lumen Gentium*, 52.
[12] Cf. ibid., 58

Nor is it just a question of the Virgin Mother's life-story, of her personal journey of faith and "the better part" which is hers in the mystery of salvation; it is also a question of the history of the whole People of God, *of all those who take part* in the same *"pilgrimage of faith"*.

The Council expresses this when it states in another passage that Mary "has gone before", becoming "a model of the Church in the matter of faith, charity, and perfect union with Christ".[13] This *"going before" as a figure or model* is in reference to the intimate mystery of the Church, as she actuates and accomplishes her own saving mission by uniting in herself—as Mary did—the qualities of *mother and virgin*. She is a virgin who "keeps whole and pure the fidelity she has pledged to her Spouse" and "becomes herself a mother", for "she brings forth to a new and immortal life children who are conceived of the Holy Spirit and born of God".[14]

6. All this is accomplished in a great historical process, comparable "to a journey". *The pilgrimage of faith indicates the interior history*, that is, the story of souls. But it is also the story of all human

[13] Ibid., 63; cf. Saint Ambrose, *Expos. Evang. sec. Lucam* II, 7: *CSEL* 32/4, 45; *De Institutione Virginis*, XIV, 88–89: *PL* 16, 341.

[14] Cf. *Lumen Gentium*, 64.

beings, subject here on earth to transitoriness, and part of the historical dimension. In the following reflections we wish to concentrate first of all on the present, which in itself is not yet history, but which nevertheless is constantly forming it, also in the sense of the history of salvation. Here there opens up a broad prospect, within which the *Blessed Virgin Mary continues to "go before" the People of God*. Her exceptional pilgrimage of faith represents a constant point of reference for the Church, for individuals and for communities, for peoples and nations, and in a sense for all humanity. It is indeed difficult to encompass and measure its range.

The Council emphasizes that *the Mother of God is already the eschatological fulfillment of the Church*: "In the most holy Virgin the Church has already reached that perfection whereby she exists without spot or wrinkle" (cf. Eph 5:27); and at the same time the Council says that "the followers of Christ still strive to increase in holiness by conquering sin, and so *they raise their eyes to Mary* who shines forth to the whole community of the elect as a model of the virtues."[15] The pilgrimage of faith no longer belongs to the Mother of the Son of God: glorified at the side of her Son in heaven, Mary has already crossed the threshold between faith and that vision

[15] Ibid., 65

which is "face to face" (1 Cor 13:12). At the same time, however, in this eschatological fulfillment, Mary does not cease to be the "Star of the Sea" (*Maris Stella*)[16] for all those who are still on the journey of faith. If they lift their eyes to her from their earthly existence, they do so because "the Son whom she brought forth is he whom God placed as the first-born among many brethren (Rom 8:29)",[17] and also because "in the birth and development" of these brothers and sisters "she cooperates with a maternal love".[18]

[16] "Take away this star of the sun which illuminates the world: where does the day go? Take away Mary, this Star of the Sea, of the great and boundless sea: what is left but a vast obscurity and the shadow of death and deepest darkness?": Saint Bernard, *In Nativitate B. Mariae Sermo—De aquaeductu*, 6: *S. Bernardi Opera*, V, 1968, 279; cf. *In laudibus Virginis Matris Homilia* II, 17: ed. cit., IV, 1966, 34f.

[17] *Lumen Gentium*, 63.

[18] Ibid., 63.

CHAPTER ONE

MARY IN THE MYSTERY OF CHRIST

1. *Full of grace*

7. "Blessed be the God and Father of our Lord Jesus Christ, who has blessed us in Christ with every spiritual blessing in the heavenly places" (Eph 1:3). These words of the Letter to the Ephesians reveal the eternal design of God the Father, his plan of man's salvation in Christ. It is a universal plan, which concerns all men and women created in the image and likeness of God (cf. Gen 1:26). Just as all are included in the creative work of God "in the beginning", so all are eternally included in the divine plan of salvation, which is to be completely revealed, in the "fullness of time", with the final coming of Christ. In fact, the God who is the "Father of our Lord Jesus Christ"— these are the next words of the same Letter—"*chose us* in him *before the foundation of the world*, that we should be holy and blameless before him. He destined us in love to be his sons through Jesus Christ, according to the purpose of his will, to the praise of his glorious grace which he freely be-

stowed on us in *the Beloved*. In him we have redemption through his Blood, the forgiveness of our trespasses, according to the riches of his grace" (Eph 1:4–7).

The divine plan of salvation—which was fully revealed to us with the coming of Christ—is eternal. And according to the teaching contained in the Letter just quoted and in other Pauline Letters (cf. Col 1:12–14; Rom 3:24; Gal 3:13; 2 Cor 5:18–29), it is also *eternally linked to Christ*. It includes everyone, but it reserves a special place for the *"woman"* who is the Mother of him to whom the Father has entrusted the work of salvation.[19] As the Second Vatican Council says, "she is already prophetically foreshadowed in that promise made to our first parents after their fall into sin"—according to the Book of Genesis (cf. 3:15). "Likewise she is the Virgin who is to conceive and bear a son, whose name will be called Emmanuel"—according to the words of Isaiah (cf. 7:14).[20] In this way the Old Testament pre-

[19] Concerning the predestination of Mary, cf. Saint John Damascene, *Hom. in Nativitatem*, 7; 10: *S. Ch.* 80, 65; 73; *Hom. in Dormitionem* I, 3: *S. Ch.* 80, 85: "For it is she, who, chosen from the ancient generations, by virtue of the predestination and benevolence of the God and Father who generated you (the Word of God) outside time without coming out of himself or suffering change, it is she who gave you birth nourished of her flesh, in the last time. . . ."

[20] *Lumen Gentium*, 55.

pares that "fullness of time" when God "sent
forth his Son, born of woman . . . so that we
might receive adoption as sons". The coming into
the world of the Son of God is an event recorded in
the first chapters of the Gospels according to Luke
and Matthew.

8. Mary is definitively *introduced into the mystery of
Christ through* this event: *the Annunciation* by the
angel. This takes place at Nazareth, within the
concrete circumstances of the history of Israel, the
people which first received God's promises. The
divine messenger says to the Virgin: "Hail, full of
grace, the Lord is with you" (Lk 1:28). Mary "was
greatly troubled at the saying, and considered in
her mind what sort of greeting this might be"
(Lk 1:29): what could those extraordinary words
mean, and in particular the expression "full of
grace" (*kecharitoméne*).[21]

[21] In Patristic tradition there is a wide and varied inter-
pretation of this expression: cf. Origen, *In Lucam Homiliae*,
VI, 7: *S. Ch.* 87, 148; Severianus of Gabala, *In mundi creationem*,
Oratio VI, 10: *PG* 56, 497f.; Saint John Chrysostom (Pseudo),
In Annuntiationem Deiparae et contra Arium impium, *PG* 62,
765f.; Basil of Seleucia, *Oratio 39, In Sanctissimae Deiparae
Annuntiationem*, 5: *PG* 85, 441–46; Antipater of Bosra, *Hom. II*,
In Sanctissimae Deiparae Annuntiationem, 3–11: *PG* 85, 1777–83;
Saint Sophronius of Jerusalem, *Oratio II, In Sanctissimae Deiparae
Annuntiationem*, 17–19: *PG* 87/3, 3235–40; Saint John Damascene,
Hom. in Dormitionem, I, 70: *S. Ch.* 80, 96–101; Saint Jerome,

If we wish to meditate together with Mary on these words, and especially on the expression "full of grace", we can find a significant echo in the very passage from the Letter to the Ephesians quoted above. And if after the announcement of the heavenly messenger the Virgin of Nazareth is also called "blessed among women" (cf. Lk 1:42), it is because of that blessing with which "God the Father" has filled us "in the heavenly places, in Christ". It is a *spiritual blessing* which is meant for all people and which bears in itself fullness and universality ("every blessing"). It flows from that love which, in the Holy Spirit, unites the con-substantial Son to the Father. At the same time, it is a blessing poured out through Jesus Christ upon human history until the end: upon all people. This blessing however refers *to Mary in a special and exceptional degree*: for she was greeted by Elizabeth as "blessed among women".

The double greeting is due to the fact that in the soul of this "daughter of Zion" there is mani-fested, in a sense, all the "glory of grace", that

Epistola 65, 9: *PL* 22, 628; Saint Ambrose, *Expos. Evang. sec. Lucam*, II, 9: *CSEL* 32/4, 45f.; Saint Augustine, *Sermo* 291, 4–6: *PL* 38, 1318f.: *Enchiridion*, 36, 11: *PL* 40, 250; Saint Peter Chrysologus, *Sermo* 142: *PL* 52, 579f.: *Sermo* 143: *PL* 52, 583; Saint Fulgentius of Ruspe, *Epistola* 17, VI, 12: *PL* 65, 458; Saint Bernard, *In laudibus Virginis Matris, Homilia III*, 2–3: *S. Bernardi Opera*, IV, 1966, 36–38.

grace which "the Father . . . has given us in his beloved Son". For the messenger greets Mary as "full of grace"; he calls her thus as if it were her real name. He does not call her by her proper earthly name: Miryam (= Mary), but *by this new name*: *"full of grace"*. What does this name mean? Why does the archangel address the Virgin of Nazareth in this way?

In the language of the Bible "grace" means a special gift, which according to the New Testament has its source precisely in the Trinitarian life of God himself, God who is love (cf. 1 Jn 4:8). The fruit of this love is *"the election"* of which the Letter to the Ephesians speaks. On the part of God, this election is the eternal desire to save man through a sharing in his own life (cf. 2 Pet 1:4) in Christ: it is salvation through a sharing in supernatural life. The effect of this eternal gift, of this grace of man's election by God, is like a *seed of holiness*, or a spring which rises in the soul as a gift from God himself, who through grace gives life and holiness to those who are chosen. In this way there is fulfilled, that is to say there comes about, that "blessing" of man "with every spiritual blessing", that "being his adopted sons and daughters . . . in Christ", in him who is eternally the "beloved Son" of the Father.

When we read that the messenger addresses Mary as "full of grace", the Gospel context, which mingles revelations and ancient promises, enables us to understand that among all the "spiritual blessings in Christ" this is a special "blessing". In the mystery of Christ she is *present* even "before the creation of the world", as the one whom the Father "has chosen" *as Mother* of his Son in the Incarnation. And, what is more, together with the Father, the Son has chosen her, entrusting her eternally to the Spirit of holiness. In an entirely special and exceptional way Mary is united to Christ, and similarly she *is eternally loved in this "beloved Son"*, this Son who is of one being with the Father, in whom is concentrated all the "glory of grace". At the same time, she is and remains perfectly open to this "gift from above" (cf. James 1:17). As the Council teaches, Mary "stands out among the poor and humble of the Lord, who confidently await and receive salvation from him".[22]

9. If the greeting and the name "full of grace" say all this, in the context of the angel's announcement they refer first of all *to the election of Mary as Mother of the Son of God*. But at the same time the "fullness of grace" indicates all the supernatural munificence from which Mary benefits by being chosen and destined to be the Mother of Christ. If this election

[22] *Lumen Gentium*, 55.

is fundamental for the accomplishment of God's salvific designs for humanity, and if the eternal choice in Christ and the vocation to the dignity of adopted children is the destiny of everyone, then the election of Mary is wholly exceptional and unique. Hence also the singularity and uniqueness of her place in the mystery of Christ.

The divine messenger says to her: "Do not be afraid, Mary, for you have found favor with God. And behold, you will conceive in your womb and bear a son, and you shall call his name Jesus. He will be great, and will be called the Son of the Most High" (Lk 1:30–32). And when the Virgin, disturbed by that extraordinary greeting asks: "How shall this be, since I have no husband?", she receives from the angel the confirmation and ex-planation of the preceding words. Gabriel says to her: "*The Holy Spirit will come upon you*, and the power of the Most High will overshadow you; therefore the child to be born will be called holy, the Son of God" (Lk 1:35).

The Annunciation, therefore, is the revelation of the mystery of the Incarnation at the very beginning of its fulfillment on earth. God's salvific giving of himself and his life, in some way to all creation but directly to man, reaches *one of its high points in the mystery of the Incarnation*. This is indeed a high point among all the gifts of grace conferred in the history of man and of the universe: Mary is "full of grace", because it is precisely in her that the Incarnation of the Word, the hypostatic union of the Son of God with human nature, is accomplished and fulfilled. As the Council says, Mary is "the Mother of the Son of God". As a result she is also the favorite daughter of the Father and the temple of the Holy Spirit. Because of this gift of sublime grace she far surpasses all other creatures, both in heaven and on earth.[23]

10. The Letter to the Ephesians, speaking of the "glory of grace" that "God, the Father . . . has bestowed on us in his beloved Son", adds: "In him we have redemption through his Blood" (Eph 1:7). According to the belief formulated in solemn documents of the Church, this "glory of grace" is manifested in the Mother of God through the fact that she has been "redeemed in a more sublime manner".[24] By virtue of the richness of the grace of the beloved Son, by reason of the redemptive merits of him who willed to become her Son, Mary was *preserved from the inheritance of original sin.*[25] In this way, from the first moment of her conception—which is to say of her existence—she belonged to Christ, sharing in salvific and sanc-

[23] Ibid., 53.

[24] Cf. Pope Pius IX, Apostolic Letter *Ineffabilis Deus* (December 8, 1854): *Pii IX P.M. Acta*, pars I, 616; *Lumen Gentium*, 53.

[25] Cf. Saint Germanus of Constantinople, *In Annuntiationem SS. Deiparae Hom.*: *PG* 98, 327f.: Saint Andrew of Crete,

tifying grace and in that love which has its beginning in the "Beloved", the Son of the Eternal
Father, who through the Incarnation became her
own Son. Consequently, through the power of
the Holy Spirit, in the order of grace, which is a
participation in the divine nature, *Mary receives life
from him to whom* she herself, in the order of earthly
generation, *gave life* as a mother. The liturgy
does not hesitate to call her "mother of her
Creator"[26] and to hail her with the words which
Dante Alighieri places on the lips of Saint Bernard:
"daughter of your Son".[27] And since Mary receives this "new life" with a fullness corresponding
to the Son's love for the Mother, and thus corresponding to the dignity of the divine motherhood, the angel at the Annunciation calls her "full
of grace".

11. In the salvific design of the Most Holy Trinity,
the mystery of the Incarnation constitutes the super-

Canon in B. Mariae Natalem, 4: *PG* 97, 1321f.; *In Nativitatem
B. Mariae*, I: *PG* 97, 811f.; *Hom. in Dormitionem S. Mariae* 1:
PG 97, 1067f.

[26] *Liturgy of the Hours* of August 15th, Assumption of the
Blessed Virgin Mary, Hymn at First and Second Vespers;
Saint Peter Damian, *Carmina et preces*, XLVII: *PL* 145, 934.

[27] *Divina Commedia*, *Paradiso*, XXXIII, 1; cf. *Liturgy of the
Hours*, Memorial of the Blessed Virgin Mary on Saturday,
Hymn II in the Office of Readings.

abundant *fulfillment of the promise* made by God to man *after original sin*, after that first sin whose effects oppress the whole earthly history of man (cf. Gen 3:15). And so, there comes into the world a Son, "the seed of the woman" who will crush the evil of sin in its very origins: "he will crush the head of the serpent". As we see from the words of the Protogospel, the victory of the woman's Son will not take place without a hard struggle, a struggle that is to extend through the whole of human history. The "enmity", foretold at the beginning, is confirmed in the Apocalypse (the book of the final events of the Church and the world), in which there recurs the Sign of the "Woman", this time "clothed with the sun" (Rev 12:1).

Mary, Mother of the Incarnate Word, is placed *at the very center of that enmity*, that struggle which accompanies the history of humanity on earth and the history of salvation itself. In this central place, she who belongs to the "weak and poor of the Lord" bears in herself, like no other member of the human race, that "glory of grace" which the Father "has bestowed on us in his beloved Son", and this *grace determines the extraordinary greatness and beauty* of her whole being. Mary thus remains before God, and also before the whole of humanity, as the unchangeable and inviolable sign of God's election, spoken of in Paul's Letter: "in Christ . . .

he chose us . . . before the foundation of the world, . . . He destined us . . . to be his sons" (Eph 1:4, 5). This election is more powerful than any experience of evil and of sin, than all that "enmity" which marks the history of man. In this history Mary remains a sign of sure hope.

2. *Blessed is she who believed*

12. Immediately after the narration of the Annunciation, the Evangelist Luke guides us in the footsteps of the Virgin of Nazareth toward "a city of Judah" (Lk 1:39). According to scholars this city would be the modern Ain Karim, situated in the mountains, not far from Jerusalem. Mary arrived there "in haste", *to visit Elizabeth* her kinswoman. The reason for her visit is also to be found in the fact that at the Annunciation Gabriel had made special mention of Elizabeth, who in her old age had conceived a son by her husband Zechariah, through the power of God: "your kinswoman Elizabeth in her old age has also conceived a son; and this is the sixth month with her who was called barren. *For with God nothing will be impossible*" (Lk 1:36–37). The divine messenger had spoken of what had been accomplished in Elizabeth in order to answer Mary's question: "How shall this be, since I have no husband?" (Lk 1:34). It is to

come to pass precisely through the "power of the Most High", just as it happened in the case of Elizabeth, and even more so.

Moved by charity, therefore, Mary goes to the house of her kinswoman. When Mary enters, Elizabeth replies to her greeting and feels the child leap in her womb, and being "filled with the Holy Spirit" she *greets Mary* with a loud cry: "Blessed are you among women, and blessed is the fruit of your womb!" (cf. Lk 1:40–42). Elizabeth's exclamation or acclamation was subsequently to become part of the *Hail Mary*, as a continuation of the angel's greeting, thus becoming one of the Church's most frequently used prayers. But still more significant are the words of Elizabeth in the question which follows: "And why is this granted me, that the mother of my Lord should come to me?" (Lk 1:43). Elizabeth bears witness to Mary: she recognizes and proclaims that before her stands the Mother of the Lord, the Mother of the Messiah. The son whom Elizabeth is carrying in her womb also shares in this witness: "The babe in my womb leaped for joy" (Lk 1:44). This child is the future John the Baptist, who at the Jordan will point out Jesus as the Messiah.

While every word of Elizabeth's greeting is filled with meaning, her final words would seem to have *fundamental importance*: "And blessed is she who believed that there would be a fulfillment of what was spoken to her from the Lord" (Lk 1:45).[28] These words can be linked with the title "full of grace" of the angel's greeting. Both of these texts reveal an essential Mariological content, namely the truth about Mary who has become really present in the mystery of Christ precisely because she "has believed". The *fullness of grace* announced by the angel means the gift of God himself. *Mary's faith*, proclaimed by Elizabeth at the Visitation, indicates *how* the Virgin of Nazareth *responded to this gift*.

13. As the Council teaches, " 'The obedience of faith' (Rom 16:26; cf. Rom 1:5; 2 Cor 10:5–6) must be given to God who reveals, an obedience by which man entrusts his whole self freely to God."[29] This description of faith found perfect realization in Mary. The "decisive" moment was the Annunciation, and the very words of Elizabeth: "And blessed is she who believed" refer primarily to that very moment.[30]

[28] Cf. Saint Augustine, *De Sancta Virginitate*, III, 3: *PL* 40, 398; *Sermo* 25, 7: *PL* 46, 937f.

[29] Second Vatican Ecumenical Council, Dogmatic Constitution on Divine Revelation *Dei Verbum*, 5.

[30] This is a classic theme, already expounded by Saint Irenaeus: "And, as by the action of the disobedient virgin, man was afflicted and, being cast down, died, so also by the action of the Virgin who obeyed the word of God, man being regenerated received, through life, life. . . . For it was meet

Indeed, at the Annunciation Mary entrusted herself to God completely, with the "full submission of intellect and will", manifesting "the obedience of faith" to him who spoke to her through his messenger.[31] She responded, therefore, *with all her human and feminine "I"*, and this response of faith included both perfect cooperation with "the grace of God that precedes and assists" and perfect openness to the action of the Holy Spirit, who "constantly brings faith to completion by his gifts".[32]

The word of the living God, announced to Mary by the angel, referred to her: "And behold, you will conceive in your womb and bear a son" (Lk 1:31). By accepting this announcement, Mary was to become the "Mother of the Lord", and the divine mystery of the Incarnation was to be accomplished in her: "The Father of Mercies willed that the consent of the predestined Mother should precede the Incarnation."[33] And Mary gives this consent, after she has heard everything the mes-

---

and just . . . that Eve should be 'recapitulated' in Mary, so that the Virgin, becoming the advocate of the virgin, should dissolve and destroy the virginal disobedience by means of virginal obedience": *Expositio doctrinae apostolicae*, 33: *S. Ch.* 62, 83–86; cf. also *Adversus Haereses*, V, 19, 1: *S. Ch.* 248–50.

[31] *Dei Verbum*, 5.

[32] Ibid., 5; cf. *Lumen Gentium*, 56.

[33] *Lumen Gentium*, 56.

senger has to say. She says: "Behold, I am the handmaid of the Lord; let it be to me according to your word" (Lk 1:38). This *fiat* of Mary—"let it be to me"—was decisive, on the human level, for the accomplishment of the divine mystery. There is a complete harmony with the words of the Son, who, according to the Letter to the Hebrews, says to the Father as he comes into the world: "Sacrifices and offering you have not desired, but *a body you have prepared for me. . . .* Lo, I have come to do your will, O God" (Heb 10:5–7). The mystery of the Incarnation was accomplished when Mary uttered her *fiat*: "Let it be to me according to your word", which made possible, as far as it depended upon her in the divine plan, the granting of her Son's desire.

Mary uttered this *fiat in faith*. In faith she entrusted herself to God without reserve and "devoted herself totally as the handmaid of the Lord to the person and work of her Son".[34] And his Son—as the Fathers of the Church teach—she conceived in her mind before she conceived him in her womb: precisely in faith![35] Rightly therefore does Eliza-

[34] Ibid., 56.

[35] Cf. ibid., 53; Saint Augustine, *De Sancta Virginitate*, III, 3: *PL* 40, 398; *Sermo* 215, 4: *PL* 38, 1074; *Sermo* 196, 1: *PL* 38, 1019; *De peccatorum meritis et remissione*, I, 29, 57: *PL* 44, 142; *Sermo* 25, 7: *PL* 46, 937–38; Saint Leo the Great, *Tractatus* 21, *de natale Domini*, I: *CCL* 138, 86.

beth praise Mary: "And blessed is she who believed *that there would be a fulfillment* of what was spoken to her from the Lord." These words have already been fulfilled: Mary of Nazareth presents herself at the threshold of Elizabeth and Zechariah's house as the Mother of the Son of God. This is Elizabeth's joyful discovery: "The mother of my Lord comes to me!"

14. Mary's faith can also be *compared to that of Abraham*, whom Saint Paul calls "our father in faith" (cf. Rom 4:12). In the salvific economy of God's revelation, Abraham's faith constitutes the beginning of the Old Covenant; Mary's faith at the Annunciation inaugurates the New Covenant. Just as Abraham "*in hope believed against hope*, that he should become the father of many nations" (cf. Rom 4:18), so Mary, at the Annunciation, having professed her virginity ("How shall this be, since I have no husband?"), *believed* that through the power of the Most High, by the power of the Holy Spirit, she would become the Mother of God's Son in accordance with the angel's revelation: "The child to be born will be called holy, the Son of God" (Lk 1:35).

However, Elizabeth's words "And blessed is she who believed" do not apply only to that particular moment of the Annunciation. Certainly the Annunciation is the culminating moment of

Mary's faith in her awaiting of Christ, but it is also the point of departure from which her whole "journey toward God" begins, her whole pilgrimage of faith. And on this road, in an eminent and truly heroic manner—indeed with an ever greater heroism of faith—the "obedience" which she professes to the word of divine revelation will be fulfilled. Mary's "obedience of faith" during the whole of her pilgrimage will show surprising similarities to the faith of Abraham. Just like the Patriarch of the People of God, so too Mary, during the pilgrimage of her filial and maternal *fiat*, "in hope believed against hope". Especially during certain stages of this journey the blessing granted to her "who believed" will be revealed with particular vividness. To believe means "to abandon oneself" to the truth of the word of the living God, knowing and humbly recognizing "how unsearchable are his judgments and how *inscrutable his ways*" (Rom 11:33). Mary, who by the eternal will of the Most High stands, one may say, at the very center of those "inscrutable ways" and "unsearchable judgments" of God, conforms herself to them in the dim light of faith, accepting fully and with a ready heart everything that is decreed in the divine plan.

15. When at the Annunciation Mary hears of the Son whose mother she is to become and to whom

"she will give the name Jesus" (= Savior), she
also learns that "the Lord God will give to him the
throne of his father David", and that "he will
reign over the house of Jacob forever and of his
kingdom there will be no end" (Lk 1:32–33). The
hope of the whole of Israel was directed toward
this. The promised Messiah is to be "great", and
the heavenly messenger also announces that *"he
will be great"*—great both by bearing the name of
Son of the Most High and by the fact that he is to
assume the *inheritance of David*. He is therefore to
be a king, he is to reign "over the house of Jacob".
Mary had grown up in the midst of these expectations of her people: could she guess, at the moment
of the Annunciation, the vital significance of the
angel's words? And how is one to understand that
"kingdom" which "will have no end"?

Although through faith she may have per-
ceived in that instant that she was the mother
of the "Messiah-King", nevertheless she replied:
"Behold, I am the handmaid of the Lord; let it be to me
according to your word" (Lk 1:38). From the first
moment Mary possessed above all the "obedience
of faith", abandoning herself to the meaning which
was given to the words of the Annunciation by
him from whom they proceeded: God himself.

16. Later, a little further along this way of the
"obedience of faith" Mary hears *other words*: those

uttered by *Simeon* in the Temple of Jerusalem. It was now forty days after the birth of Jesus when, in accordance with the precepts of the Law of Moses, Mary and Joseph "brought him up to Jerusalem to present him to the Lord" (Lk 2:22). The birth had taken place in conditions of extreme poverty. We know from Luke that when, on the occasion of the census ordered by the Roman authorities, Mary went with Joseph to Bethlehem, having found "no place in the inn", *she gave birth to her Son in a stable* and "laid him in a manger" (cf. Lk 2:7).

A just and God-fearing man, called Simeon, appears at the beginning of Mary's "journey" of faith. His words, suggested by the Holy Spirit (cf. Lk 2:25–27), confirm the truth of the Annunciation. For we read that he took up in his arms the child to whom—in accordance with the angel's command —the name Jesus was given (cf. Lk 2:21). Simeon's words match the meaning of this name, which is Savior: "God is salvation." Turning to the Lord, he says: "For my eyes have seen your *salvation* which you have prepared *in the presence of all peoples*, a light for revelation to the Gentiles, and for glory to your people Israel" (Lk 2:30–32). At the same time, however, Simeon addresses Mary with the following words: "Behold, this child is set for the fall and rising of many in Israel, and for a *sign that is spoken against*, that thoughts out of

many hearts may be revealed"; and he adds with
direct reference to her: "and a sword will pierce
through your own soul also" (cf. Lk 2:34–35).
Simeon's words cast new light on the announcement which Mary had heard from the angel: Jesus
is the Savior, he is "*a light* for revelation" to
mankind. Is not this what was manifested, in a
way on Christmas night, when the *shepherds* came
to the stable (cf. Lk 2:8–20)? Is not this what was
manifested even more clearly in the coming of the
Magi from the East (cf. Mt 2:1–12)? But at the same
time, at the very beginning of his life, the Son of
Mary, and his Mother with him, will experience
in themselves the truth of those other words of
Simeon: "a sign that is spoken against" (Lk 2:34).
Simeon's words seem like a *second Annunciation to
Mary*, for they tell her of the actual historical
situation in which the Son is to accomplish his
mission, namely in misunderstanding and sorrow.
While this announcement on the one hand confirms her faith in the accomplishment of the divine
promises of salvation, on the other hand it also
reveals to her that she will have to live her
obedience of faith in suffering, at the side of the
suffering Savior, and that her motherhood will be
mysterious and sorrowful. Thus, after the visit of
the Magi who came from the East, after their
homage ("they fell down and worshipped him")
and after they had offered gifts (cf. Mt 2:11), Mary

together with the child *has to flee into Egypt* in the protective care of Joseph, for "Herod is about to search for the child, to destroy him" (cf. Mt 2:13). And until the death of Herod they will have to remain in Egypt (cf. Mt 2:15).

17. When the Holy Family returns to Nazareth after Herod's death, there begins the long *period of the hidden life*. She "who believed that there would be a fulfillment of what was spoken to her from the Lord" (Lk 1:45) lives the reality of these words day by day. And daily at her side is the Son to whom *"she gave the name Jesus"*; therefore in contact with him she certainly uses this name, a fact which would have surprised no one, since the name had long been in use in Israel. Nevertheless, Mary knows that he who bears the name *Jesus has been called by the angel "the Son of the Most High"* (cf. Lk 1:32). Mary knows she has conceived and given birth to him "without having a husband", by the power of the Holy Spirit, by the power of the Most High who overshadowed her (cf. Lk 1:35), just as at the time of Moses and the Patriarchs the cloud covered the presence of God (cf. Ex 24:16; 40:34–35; 1 Kings 8:10–12). Therefore Mary knows that the Son to whom she gave birth in a virginal manner is precisely that "Holy One", the Son of God, of whom the angel spoke to her.

During the years of Jesus' hidden life in the

house at Nazareth, *Mary's life* too is *"hid with Christ in God"* (cf. Col 3:3) *through faith*. For faith is contact with the mystery of God. Every day Mary is in constant contact with the ineffable mystery of God made man, a mystery that surpasses everything revealed in the Old Covenant. From the moment of the Annunciation, the mind of the Virgin-Mother has been initiated into the radical "newness" of God's self-revelation and has been made aware of the mystery. She is the first of those "little ones" of whom Jesus will say one day: "Father, . . . you have hidden these things from the wise and understanding and revealed them to babes" (Mt 11:25). For "no one knows the Son except the Father" (Mt 11:27). If this is the case, how can Mary "know the Son"? Of course she does not know him as the Father does; and yet she is *the first of those to whom the Father "has chosen to reveal him"* (cf. Mt 11:26–27; 1 Cor 2:11). If though, from the moment of the Annunciation, the Son— whom only the Father knows completely, as the one who begets him in the eternal "today" (cf. Ps 2:7)—was revealed to Mary, she, his Mother, is in contact with the truth about her Son only in faith and through faith! She is therefore blessed, because "she has believed", and continues to *believe day after day* amidst all the trials and the adversities of Jesus' infancy and then during the years of the hidden life at Nazareth, where he "was obedient

to them" (Lk 2:51). He was obedient both to Mary
and also to Joseph, since Joseph took the place of
his father in people's eyes; for this reason, the son
of Mary was regarded by the people as "the car-
penter's son" (Mt 13:55).

The Mother of *that Son*, therefore, mindful of
what has been told her at the Annunciation and in
subsequent events, bears within herself the radical
"newness" of faith: *the beginning of the New
Covenant*. This is the beginning of the Gospel, the
joyful Good News. However, it is not difficult to
see in that beginning *a particular heaviness of heart*,
linked with a sort of "night of faith"—to use the
words of Saint John of the Cross—a kind of "veil"
through which one has to draw near to the Invisible
One and to live in intimacy with the mystery.[36]
And this is the way that Mary, for many years,
lived in intimacy with the mystery of her Son, and
went forward in her "pilgrimage of faith", while
Jesus "increased in wisdom . . . and in favor with
God and man" (Lk 2:52). God's predilection for
him was manifested ever more clearly to people's
eyes. The first human creature thus permitted to
discover Christ was Mary, who lived with Joseph
in the same house at Nazareth.

However, when he had been found in the
Temple, and his Mother asked him "Son, why

[36] *Ascent of Mount Carmel*, 1, II, Ch. 3, 4–6.

have you treated us so?" the *twelve-year-old Jesus*
answered: "Did you not know that I must be in
my Father's house?" And the Evangelist adds:
"*And they* (Joseph and Mary) *did not understand* the
saying which he spoke to them" (Lk 2:48–50).
Jesus was aware that "no one knows the Son
except the Father" (cf. Mt 11:27); thus even his
Mother, to whom had been revealed most completely the mystery of his divine sonship, lived in
intimacy with this mystery only through faith!
Living side by side with her Son under the same
roof, and faithfully persevering "in her union with
her Son", she "*advanced in her pilgrimage of faith*",
as the Council emphasizes.[37] And so it was during
Christ's public life too (cf. Mk 3:21–35) that day
by day there was fulfilled in her the blessing uttered by Elizabeth at the Visitation: "Blessed is she
who believed."

18. This blessing reaches its full meaning *when
Mary stands beneath the Cross* of her Son (cf. Jn 19:25).
The Council says that this happened "not without
a divine plan": by "suffering deeply with her
only-begotten Son and joining herself with her
maternal spirit to his sacrifice, lovingly consenting
to the immolation of the victim to whom she had
given birth", in this way Mary "faithfully pre-

[37] Cf. *Lumen Gentium*, 58.

served her union with her Son even to the Cross".[38] It is a union through faith—the same faith with which she had received the angel's revelation at the Annunciation. At that moment she had also heard the words: "He will be great . . . and *the Lord God* will give to him the throne of his father David, and he will reign over the house of Jacob forever; and of his kingdom there will be no end" (Lk 1:32–33).

And now, standing at the foot of the Cross, Mary is the witness, humanly speaking, of the complete *negation of these words*. On that wood of the Cross her Son hangs in agony as one condemned. "He was despised and rejected by men; a man of sorrows . . . he was despised, and we esteemed him not": as one destroyed (cf. Is 53:3–5). How great, how heroic then is the *obedience of faith* shown by Mary in the face of God's "unsearchable judgments"! How completely she "abandons herself to God" without reserve, "offering the full assent of the intellect and the will"[39] to him whose "ways are inscrutable" (cf. Rom 11:33)! And how powerful too is the action of grace in her soul, how all-pervading is the influence of the Holy Spirit and of his light and power!

Through this faith Mary is perfectly united with

[38] Ibid., 58.
[39] Cf. *Dei Verbum*, 5.

Christ in his self-emptying. For "Christ Jesus, who, though he was in the form of God, did not count equality with God a thing to be grasped, but emptied himself, taking the form of a servant, being born in the likeness of men": precisely on Golgotha "he humbled himself and became obedient unto death, even death on a cross" (cf. Phil 2:5–8). At the foot of the Cross Mary shares through faith in the shocking mystery of this self-emptying. This is perhaps the deepest *"kenosis" of faith* in human history. Through faith the Mother shares in the death of her Son, in his redeeming death; but in contrast with the faith of the disciples who fled, hers was far more enlightened. On Golgotha, Jesus through the Cross definitively confirmed that he was the "sign of contradiction" foretold by Simeon. At the same time, there were also fulfilled on Golgotha the words which Simeon had addressed to Mary: "and a sword will pierce through your own soul also".[40]

19. Yes, truly "blessed is she who believed"! These words, spoken by Elizabeth after the Annunciation, here at the foot of the Cross seem to re-echo with supreme eloquence, and the power contained within

---

[40] Concerning Mary's participation or "compassion" in the death of Christ, cf. Saint Bernard, *In Dominica infra octavam Assumptionis Sermo*, 14: *S. Bernardi Opera*, V, 1968, 273.

them becomes something penetrating. From the Cross, that is to say from the very heart of the mystery of Redemption, there radiates and spreads out the prospect of that blessing of faith. It goes right back to "the beginning", and as a sharing in the sacrifice of Christ—the new Adam—it becomes in a certain sense *the counterpoise to the disobedience and disbelief* embodied in the sin of our first parents. Thus teach the Fathers of the Church and especially Saint Irenaeus, quoted by the Constitution *Lumen Gentium*: "The knot of Eve's disobedience was untied by Mary's obedience; what the virgin Eve bound through her unbelief, Mary *loosened by her faith*."[41] In the light of this comparison with Eve, the Fathers of the Church—as the Council also says—call Mary the "mother of the living" and often speak of "death through Eve, life through Mary".[42]

In the expression "Blessed is she who believed", we can therefore rightly find *a kind of "key"* which unlocks for us the innermost reality of Mary, whom the angel hailed as "full of grace". If as "full of grace" she has been eternally present in the mystery of Christ, through faith she became a sharer in that mystery in every extension of her

[41] Saint Irenaeus, *Adversus Haereses*, III, 22, 4: S. Ch. 211, 438–44; cf. *Lumen Gentium*, 56, note 6.

[42] Cf. *Lumen Gentium*, 56, and the Fathers quoted there in notes 8 and 9.

earthly journey. She "advanced in her pilgrimage
of faith" and at the same time, in a discreet yet
direct and effective way, she made present to
humanity *the mystery of Christ*. And she still continues to do so. Through the mystery of Christ,
she too is present within mankind. Thus through
the mystery of the Son the mystery of the Mother
is also made clear.

3. *Behold your Mother*

20. The Gospel of Luke records the moment when
"a woman in the crowd raised her voice" and said
to Jesus: *"Blessed is the womb that bore you, and the
breasts that you sucked!"* (Lk 11:27). These words
were an expression of praise of Mary as Jesus'
mother according to the flesh. Probably the
Mother of Jesus was not personally known to this
woman; in fact, when Jesus began his messianic
activity Mary did not accompany him but continued to remain at Nazareth. One could say that
the words of that unknown woman in a way
brought Mary out of her hiddenness.

Through these words, there flashed out in the
midst of the crowd, at least for an instant, the
gospel of Jesus' infancy. This is the gospel in
which Mary is present as the mother who con-
ceives Jesus in her womb, gives him birth and
nurses him: the nursing mother referred to by the

woman in the crowd. *Thanks to this motherhood, Jesus*, the Son of the Most High (cf. Lk 1:32), is a true *son of man*. He is "flesh", like every other man: he is "the Word [who] became flesh" (cf. Jn 1:14). He is of the flesh and blood of Mary![43]

But to the blessing uttered by that woman upon her who was his mother according to the flesh, Jesus replies in a significant way: "Blessed rather are *those who hear the word of God and keep it*" (Lk 11:28). He wishes to divert attention from motherhood understood only as a fleshly bond, in order to direct it toward those mysterious bonds of the spirit which develop from hearing and keeping God's word.

This same shift into the sphere of spiritual values is seen even more clearly in another response of Jesus reported by all the Synoptics. When Jesus is told that "his mother and brothers are standing outside and wish to see him", he replies: "*My mother and my brothers are those who hear the word of God and do it*" (cf. Lk 8:20–21). This he said "looking around on those who sat about him", as we read in Mark (3:34) or, according to Matthew (12:49), "stretching out his hand toward his disciples".

These statements seem to *fit in with the reply*

[43] "Christ is truth, Christ is flesh: Christ truth in the mind of Mary, Christ flesh in the womb of Mary": Saint Augustine, *Sermo* 25 (*Sermones inediti*), 7: *PL* 46, 938.

which the twelve-year-old Jesus gave to Mary and
Joseph when he was found after three days in the
Temple at Jerusalem.

Now, when Jesus left Nazareth and began his
public life throughout Palestine, *he was completely
and exclusively "concerned with his Father's business"*
(cf. Lk 2:49). He announced the kingdom: the
"kingdom of God" and "his Father's business",
which add a new dimension and meaning to everything human, and therefore to every human bond,
insofar as these things relate to the goals and tasks
assigned to every human being. Within this new
dimension, also a bond such as that of "brotherhood" means something different from "brotherhood according to the flesh" deriving from a
common origin from the same set of parents.
"Motherhood" too, *in the dimension of the kingdom of
God and in the radius of the fatherhood of God himself,
takes on another meaning*. In the words reported by
Luke, Jesus teaches precisely this new meaning of
motherhood.

Is Jesus thereby distancing himself from his
mother according to the flesh? Does he perhaps
wish to leave her in the hidden obscurity which
she herself has chosen? If this seems to be the case
from the tone of those words, one must nevertheless note that the new and different motherhood which Jesus speaks of to his disciples refers
precisely to Mary in a very special way. Is not

Mary *the first of "those who hear the word of God and do it"*? And therefore does not the blessing uttered by Jesus in response to the woman in the crowd refer primarily to her? Without any doubt, Mary is worthy of blessing by the very fact that she became the mother of Jesus according to the flesh ("Blessed is the womb that bore you, and the breasts that you sucked"), but also and especially because already at the Annunciation she accepted the word of God, because she believed it, *because she was obedient to God*, and because she "kept" the word and "pondered it in her heart" (cf. Lk 1:38, 45; 2:19, 51) and by means of her whole life accomplished it. Thus we can say that the blessing proclaimed by Jesus is not in opposition, despite appearances, to the blessing uttered by the unknown woman, but rather coincides with that blessing in the person of this Virgin Mother, who called herself only "the handmaid of the Lord" (Lk 1:38). If it is true that "all generations will call her blessed" (cf. Lk 1:48), then it can be said that the unnamed woman was the first to confirm unwittingly that prophetic phrase of Mary's *Magnificat* and to begin the *Magnificat* of the ages.

If *through faith* Mary became the bearer of the Son given to her by the Father through the power of the Holy Spirit, while preserving her virginity intact, in that same faith she *discovered and accepted the other dimension of motherhood* revealed by Jesus during his messianic mission. One can say that this dimension of motherhood belonged to Mary from the beginning, that is to say from the moment of the conception and birth of her Son. From that time she was "the one who believed". But as the messianic mission of her Son grew clearer to her eyes and spirit, she herself as a mother became ever more open *to that new dimension of motherhood* which was to constitute her "part" beside her Son. Had she not said from the very beginning: "Behold, I am the handmaid of the Lord; let it be to me according to your word" (Lk 1:38)? Through faith Mary continued to hear and to ponder that word, in which there became ever clearer, in a way "which surpasses knowledge" (Eph 3:19), the self-revelation of the living God. Thus *in a sense* Mary as Mother became *the first "disciple" of her Son*, the first to whom he seemed to say: "Follow me", even before he addressed this call to the Apostles or to anyone else (cf. Jn 1:43).

21. From this point of view, particularly eloquent is the passage in the *Gospel of John* which presents Mary at the wedding feast of Cana. She appears there as the Mother of Jesus at the beginning of his public life: "There was *a marriage at Cana in Galilee*, and the mother of Jesus was there; Jesus also was invited to the marriage, with his disciples" (Jn 2:1–2).

From the text it appears that Jesus and his disciples were invited together with Mary, as if by reason of her presence at the celebration: the Son seems to have been invited because of his Mother. We are familiar with the sequence of events which resulted from that invitation, that "beginning of the signs" wrought by Jesus—the water changed into wine—which prompts the Evangelist to say that Jesus "manifested his glory; and his disciples believed in him" (Jn 2:11).

Mary is present at Cana in Galilee as the *Mother of Jesus*, and in a significant way she *contributes* to that "beginning of the signs" which reveal the messianic power of her Son. We read: "When the wine gave out, the mother of Jesus said to him, 'They have no wine.' And Jesus said to her, 'O woman, what have you to do with me? My hour has not yet come' "(Jn 2:3–4). In John's Gospel that "hour" means the time appointed by the Father when the Son accomplishes his tasks and is to be glorified (cf. Jn 7:30; 8:20; 12:23, 27; 13:1; 17:1; 19:27). Even though Jesus' reply to his Mother sounds like a refusal (especially if we consider the blunt statement "My hour has not yet come" rather than the question), Mary nevertheless turns to the servants and says to them: "Do whatever he tells you" (Jn 2:5). Then Jesus orders the servants to fill the stone jars with water, and the water becomes wine, better than the wine which has previously been served to the wedding guests.

What deep understanding existed between Jesus and his Mother? How can we probe the mystery of their intimate spiritual union? But the fact speaks for itself. It is certain that that event already quite clearly outlines *the new dimension*, the new meaning *of Mary's motherhood*. Her motherhood has a significance which is not exclusively contained in the words of Jesus and in the various episodes reported by the Synoptics (Lk 11:27–28 and Lk 8:19–21; Mt 12:46–50; Mk 3:31–35). In these texts Jesus means above all to contrast the motherhood resulting from the fact of birth with what this "motherhood" (and also "brotherhood") is to be in the dimension of the kingdom of God, in the salvific radius of God's fatherhood. In John's text on the other hand, the description of the Cana event outlines what is actually manifested as a new kind of motherhood according to the spirit and not just according to the flesh, that is to say *Mary's solicitude for human beings*, her coming to them in the wide variety of their wants and needs. At Cana in Galilee there is shown only one concrete aspect of human need, apparently a small one and of little importance ("They have no wine"). But it has a symbolic value: this coming to the aid of human needs means, at the same time, bringing those needs within the radius of Christ's messianic mission and salvific power. Thus there is a mediation: Mary places herself between her Son and mankind in the reality of their wants, needs, and sufferings. *She puts herself "in the middle"*, that is to say *she acts as a mediatrix not as an outsider, but in her position as mother*. She knows that as such she can point out to her Son the needs of mankind, and in fact, she "has the right" to do so. Her mediation is thus in the nature of intercession: Mary "intercedes" for mankind. And that is not all. As a mother she also *wishes the messianic power of her Son to be manifested*, that salvific power of his which is meant to help man in his misfortunes, to free him from the evil which in various forms and degrees weighs heavily upon his life. Precisely as the Prophet Isaiah had foretold about the Messiah in the famous passage which Jesus quoted before his fellow townsfolk in Nazareth: "To preach good news to the poor . . . to proclaim release to the captives and recovering of sight to the blind . . ." (cf. Lk 4:18).

Another essential element of Mary's maternal task is found in her words to the servants: "Do whatever he tells you." *The Mother* of Christ presents herself as the *spokeswoman of her Son's will*, pointing out those things which must be done so that the salvific power of the Messiah may be manifested. At Cana, thanks to the intercession of Mary and the obedience of the servants, Jesus begins "his hour". At Cana Mary appears as *believing in Jesus*. Her faith evokes his first "sign" and helps to kindle the faith of the disciples.

22. We can therefore say that in this passage of John's Gospel we find as it were a first manifestation of the truth concerning Mary's maternal care. This truth has also found expression *in the teaching of the Second Vatican Council*. It is important to note how the Council illustrates Mary's maternal role as it relates to the mediation of Christ. Thus we read: "Mary's maternal function toward mankind in no way obscures or diminishes the unique mediation of Christ, but rather shows its efficacy", because "there is one mediator between God and men, the man Christ Jesus" (1 Tim 2:5). This maternal role of Mary flows, according to God's good pleasure, "from the superabundance of the merits of Christ; it is founded on his mediation, absolutely depends on it, and draws all its efficacy from it."[44] It is precisely in this sense that the episode at Cana in Galilee offers us *a sort of first announcement of Mary's mediation*, wholly oriented toward Christ and tending to the revelation of his salvific power.

From the *text of John* it is evident that it is a mediation which is maternal. As the Council proclaims: Mary became "a mother to us in the order

[44] *Lumen Gentium*, 60.

of grace". This motherhood in the order of grace flows from her divine motherhood. Because she was, by the design of divine Providence, the mother who nourished the divine Redeemer, Mary became "an associate of unique nobility, and the Lord's humble handmaid", who "cooperated by her obedience, faith, hope, and burning charity in the Savior's work of restoring supernatural life to souls".[45] And "this *maternity of Mary in the order of grace* . . . will last without interruption until the eternal fulfillment of all the elect".[46]

23. If John's description of the event at Cana presents Mary's caring motherhood at the beginning of Christ's messianic activity, another passage from the same Gospel confirms this motherhood in the salvific economy of grace at its crowning moment, namely when Christ's sacrifice on the Cross, his Paschal Mystery, is accomplished. John's description is concise: "*Standing by the cross of Jesus* were his mother, and his mother's sister, Mary the wife of Clopas, and Mary Magdalen. When Jesus saw his mother, and the disciple whom he loved standing near, he said to his mother: 'Woman, behold your son!' Then he said to the disciple, 'Behold, your mother!' And from

[45] Ibid., 61.
[46] Ibid., 62.

that hour the disciple took her to his own home" (Jn 19:25–27).

Undoubtedly, we find here an expression of the Son's particular solicitude for his Mother, whom he is leaving in such great sorrow. And yet the "testament of Christ's Cross" says more. Jesus highlights a new relationship between Mother and Son, the whole truth and reality of which he solemnly confirms. One can say that if Mary's motherhood of the human race had already been outlined, now it is clearly stated and established. It *emerges* from the definitive accomplishment of *the Redeemer's Paschal Mystery*. The Mother of Christ, who stands at the very center of this mystery—a mystery which embraces each individual and all humanity—is given as mother to every single individual and all mankind. The man at the foot of the Cross is John, "the disciple whom he loved".[47] But it is not he alone. Following Tradition, the Council does not hesitate to call Mary "*the Mother of Christ and mother of mankind*": since she "belongs to the offspring of Adam she is one with all human

[47] There is a well-known passage of Origen on the presence of Mary and John on Calvary: "The Gospels are the first fruits of all Scripture and the Gospel of John is the first of the Gospels: no one can grasp its meaning without having leaned his head on Jesus' breast and having received from Jesus Mary as Mother": *Comm. in Ioan.*, I, 6: *PG* 14, 31; cf. Saint Ambrose, *Expos. Evang. sec. Lucam*, X, 129–31: *CSEL* 32/4, 504f.

beings. . . . Indeed she is 'clearly the mother of the members of Christ . . . since she cooperated out of love so that there might be born in the Church the faithful' ".[48]

And so this "new motherhood of Mary", generated by faith, is *the fruit of the "new" love* which came to definitive maturity in her at the foot of the Cross, through her sharing in the redemptive love of her Son.

24. Thus we find ourselves at the very center of the fulfillment of the promise contained in the Protogospel: the "seed of the woman . . . will crush the head of the serpent" (cf. Gen 3:15). By his redemptive death Jesus Christ conquers the evil of sin and death at its very roots. It is significant that, as he speaks to his Mother from the Cross, he calls her "woman" and says to her: "Woman, behold your son!" Moreover, he had addressed her by the same term at Cana too (cf. Jn 2:4). How can one doubt that especially now, on Golgotha, this expression goes to the very heart of the mystery of Mary, and indicates the unique *place* which she occupies *in the whole economy of salvation*? As the Council teaches, in Mary "the exalted Daughter of Zion, and after a

---

[48] *Lumen Gentium*, 54 and 53; the latter text quotes Saint Augustine, *De Sancta Virginitate*, VI, 6: *PL* 40, 399.

long expectation of the promise, the times were at
length fulfilled and the new dispensation established. All this occurred when the Son of God
took a human nature from her, that he might in
the mysteries of his flesh free man from sin."[49]

The words uttered by Jesus from the Cross
signify that *the motherhood* of her who bore Christ
finds a "new" continuation *in the Church and through
the Church*, symbolized and represented by John.
In this way, she who as the one "full of grace" was
brought into the mystery of Christ in order to be
his Mother and thus *the Holy Mother of God*, through
the Church remains in that mystery *as "the woman"*
spoken of by the Book of Genesis (3:15) at the
beginning and by the Apocalypse (12:1) at the end
of the history of salvation. In accordance with the
eternal plan of Providence, Mary's divine motherhood is to be poured out upon the Church, as
indicated by statements of Tradition, according to
which Mary's "motherhood" of the Church is the
reflection and extension of the motherhood of the
Son of God.[50]

According to the Council, the very moment of
the Church's birth and full manifestation to the
world enables us to glimpse this continuity of
Mary's motherhood: "Since it pleased God not to

[49] *Lumen Gentium*, 55.

[50] Cf. Saint Leo the Great, *Tractatus 26, de natale Domini*, 2:
CCL 138, 126.

manifest solemnly the mystery of the salvation of the human race until he poured forth the Spirit promised by Christ, we see the *Apostles* before the day of Pentecost 'continuing with one mind *in prayer* with the women and *Mary the mother of Jesus*, and with his brethren' (Acts 1:14). We see Mary prayerfully imploring the gift of the Spirit, who had already overshadowed her in the Annunciation."[51]

And so, in the redemptive economy of grace, brought about through the action of the Holy Spirit, there is a unique correspondence between the moment of the Incarnation of the Word and the moment of the birth of the Church. The person who links these two moments is Mary: *Mary at Nazareth* and *Mary in the Upper Room at Jerusalem*. In both cases her discreet yet essential presence indicates the path of "birth from the Holy Spirit". Thus she who is present in the mystery of Christ as Mother becomes—by the will of the Son and the power of the Holy Spirit—present in the mystery of the Church. In the Church too she continues to be *a maternal presence*, as is shown by the words spoken from the Cross: "Woman, behold your son!"; "Behold, your mother."

[51] *Lumen Gentium*, 59.

CHAPTER TWO

THE MOTHER OF GOD AT THE CENTER OF THE PILGRIM CHURCH

1. *The Church, the People of God present in all the nations of the earth*

25. "The Church 'like a pilgrim in a foreign land, presses forward amid the persecutions of the world and the consolations of God'[52], announcing the Cross and Death of the Lord until he comes (cf. 1 Cor 11:26)."[53] "Israel according to the flesh, which wandered as an exile in the desert, was already called the Church of God (cf. 2 Esd 13:1; Num 20:4; Dt 23:1ff.). Likewise the new Israel . . . is also called the Church of Christ (cf. Mt 16:18). For he has bought it for himself with his Blood (Acts 20:28), has filled it with his Spirit, and provided it with those means which befit it as a visible and social unity. *God has gathered together as one all those who in faith look upon Jesus* as the author of salvation and the source of unity and peace, and

[52] Saint Augustine, *De Civitate Dei*, XVIII, 51: *CCL*, 48, 650.
[53] *Lumen Gentium*, 8.

has established them as the Church, that for each and all she may be the visible sacrament of this saving unity."[54]

The Second Vatican Council speaks of the pilgrim Church, establishing an analogy with the Israel of the Old Covenant journeying through the desert. The journey also has an *external character*, visible in the time and space in which it historically takes place. For the Church "is destined to extend to all regions of the earth and so to enter into the history of mankind", but at the same time "she transcends all limits of time and of space".[55] And yet the essential *character* of her pilgrimage is *interior*: it is a question of a *pilgrimage through faith*, by "the power of the Risen Lord",[56] a pilgrimage in the Holy Spirit, given to the Church as the invisible Comforter (*paráklētos*) (cf. Jn 14:26; 15:26; 16:7): "Moving forward through trial and tribulation, the Church is strengthened by the power of God's grace promised to her by the Lord, so that . . . moved by the Holy Spirit she may never cease to renew herself, until through the Cross she arrives at the light which knows no setting."[57]

It is precisely *in this ecclesial journey or pilgrimage* through space and time, and even more through

[54] Ibid., 9.
[55] Ibid., 9.
[56] Ibid., 8.
[57] Ibid., 9.

the history of souls, that *Mary is present*, as the one who is "blessed because she believed", as the one who advanced on the pilgrimage of faith, sharing unlike any other creature in the mystery of Christ. The Council further says that "Mary figured profoundly in the history of salvation and in a certain way unites and mirrors within herself the central truths of the Faith."[58] Among all believers she is *like a "mirror"* in which are reflected in the most profound and limpid way "the mighty works of God" (Acts 2:11).

26. Built by Christ upon the Apostles, the Church became fully aware of these mighty works of God *on the day of Pentecost*, when those gathered together in the Upper Room "were all filled with the Holy Spirit and began to speak in other tongues, as the Spirit gave them utterance" (Acts 2:4). From that moment there also *begins* that journey of faith, *the Church's pilgrimage* through the history of individuals and peoples. We know that at the beginning of this journey Mary is present. We see her in the midst of the Apostles in the Upper Room, "prayerfully imploring the gift of the Spirit".[59]

In a sense her journey of faith is longer. The

[58] Ibid., 65.
[59] Ibid., 59.

Holy Spirit had already come down upon her, and she became his faithful spouse *at the Annunciation*, welcoming the Word of the true God, offering "the full submission of intellect and will . . . and freely assenting to the truth revealed by him", indeed abandoning herself totally to God through "the obedience of faith",[60] whereby she replied to the angel: "Behold, I am the handmaid of the Lord; let it be to me according to your word." The journey of faith made by Mary, whom we see praying in the Upper Room, is thus longer than that of the others gathered there. Mary "goes before them", "leads the way" for them.[61] *The moment of Pentecost* in Jerusalem had been prepared for by the *moment of the Annunciation* in Nazareth, as well as by the Cross. In the Upper Room Mary's journey meets the Church's journey of faith. In what way?

Among those who devoted themselves to prayer in the Upper Room, preparing to go "into the whole world" after receiving the Spirit, some *had been called by Jesus* gradually from the beginning of his mission in Israel. Eleven of them *had been made Apostles*, and to them Jesus had passed on the mission which he himself had received from the Father. "As the Father has sent me, even so I send

[60] Cf. *Dei Verbum*, 5.
[61] Cf. *Lumen Gentium*, 63.

you" (Jn 20:21), he had said to the Apostles after the Resurrection. And forty days later, before returning to the Father, he had added: "when the Holy Spirit has come upon you . . . *you shall be my witnesses* . . . to the end of the earth" (cf. Acts 1:8). This mission of the Apostles began the moment they left the Upper Room in Jerusalem. The Church is born and then grows through the testimony that Peter and the Apostles bear to the Crucified and Risen Christ (cf. Acts 2:31–34; 3:15–18; 4:10–12; 5:30–32).

Mary did not directly receive this apostolic mission. She was not among those whom Jesus sent "to the whole world to teach all nations" (cf. Mt 28:19) when he conferred this mission on them. But she was in the Upper Room, where the Apostles were preparing to take up this mission with the coming of the Spirit of Truth: she was present with them. In their midst Mary was "devoted to prayer" as the "mother of Jesus" (cf. Acts 1:13–14), of the Crucified and Risen Christ. And that first group of those who in faith looked "upon Jesus as the author of salvation",[62] knew that Jesus was the Son of Mary, and that she was his Mother, and that as such she was from the moment of his conception and birth a unique witness to *the mystery of Jesus*, that mystery which before their

[62] Cf. ibid., 9.

eyes had been disclosed and confirmed in the
Cross and Resurrection. Thus from the very first
moment the Church "looked at" Mary through
Jesus, just as she "looked at" Jesus through Mary.
For the Church of that time and of every time
Mary is a singular witness to the years of Jesus'
infancy and hidden life at Nazareth, when she
"kept all these things, pondering them in her
heart" (Lk 2:19; cf. Lk 2:51).

But above all, in the Church of that time and of
every time Mary was and is the one who is "blessed
because she believed"; *she was the first to believe*.
From the moment of the Annunciation and conception, from the moment of his birth in the stable
at Bethlehem, Mary followed Jesus step by step in
her maternal pilgrimage of faith. She followed
him during the years of his hidden life at Nazareth;
she followed him also during the time after he left
home, when he began "to do and to teach" (cf.
Acts 1:1) in the midst of Israel. Above all she
followed him in the tragic experience of Golgotha.
Now, while Mary was with the Apostles in the
Upper Room in Jerusalem at the dawn of the
Church, *her faith, born from the words of the Annunciation, found confirmation*. The angel had said to her
then: "You will conceive in your womb and bear a
son, and you shall call his name Jesus. He will be
great . . . and he will reign over the house of Jacob

forever; and of his kingdom there will be no end."
The recent events on Calvary had shrouded that
promise in darkness, yet not even beneath the
Cross did Mary's faith fail. She had still remained
the one who, like Abraham, "in hope believed
against hope" (Rom 4:18). But it is only after the
Resurrection that hope had shown its true face and
the promise had begun to be transformed into reality.
For Jesus, before returning to the Father, had said
to the Apostles: "Go therefore and make disciples
of all nations. . . . Lo, I am with you always, to
the close of the age" (cf. Mt 28:19–20). Thus had
spoken the one who by his Resurrection had
revealed himself as the conqueror of death, as the
one who possessed the kingdom of which, as the
angel said, "there will be no end".

27. Now, at the first dawn of the Church, at the
beginning of the long journey through faith which
began at Pentecost in Jerusalem, Mary was with
all those who were the seed of the "new Israel".
She was present among them as an exceptional
witness to the mystery of Christ. And the Church
was assiduous in prayer together with her, and at
the same time *"contemplated her in the light of the
Word made man"*. It was always to be so. For when
the Church "enters more intimately into the supreme mystery of the Incarnation", she thinks

of the Mother of Christ with profound reverence and devotion.[63] Mary belongs indissolubly to the mystery of Christ, and she belongs also to the mystery of the Church from the beginning, from the day of the Church's birth. At the basis of what the Church has been from the beginning, and of what she must continually become from generation to generation, in the midst of all the nations of the earth, we find the one "who believed that there would be a fulfillment of what was spoken to her from the Lord" (Lk 1:45). It is precisely Mary's faith which marks the beginning of the new and eternal Covenant of God with man in Jesus Christ; this heroic *faith* of hers *"precedes"* the apostolic *witness* of the Church, and ever remains in the Church's heart, hidden like a special heritage of God's revelation. All those who from generation to generation accept the apostolic witness of the Church share in that mysterious inheritance, and *in a sense share in Mary's faith*.

Elizabeth's words "blessed is she who believed" continue to accompany the Virgin also at Pentecost; they accompany her from age to age, wherever knowledge of Christ's salvific mystery spreads, through the Church's apostolic witness and service. Thus is fulfilled the prophecy of the *Magnificat*: "*All generations will call me blessed*; for he who is

[63] Cf. ibid., 65.

mighty has done great things for me, and holy is his name" (Lk 1:48–49). For knowledge of the mystery of Christ leads us to bless his Mother, in the form of special veneration for the *Theotókos*. But this veneration always includes a blessing of her faith, for the Virgin of Nazareth became blessed above all through this faith, in accordance with Elizabeth's words. Those who from generation to generation among the different peoples and nations of the earth accept with faith the mystery of Christ, the Incarnate Word and Redeemer of the world, not only turn with veneration to Mary and confidently have recourse to her as his Mother, but they also *seek in her faith support for their own*. And it is precisely this lively sharing in Mary's faith that determines her special place in the Church's pilgrimage as the new People of God throughout the earth.

28.   As the Council says, "Mary figured profoundly in the history of salvation. . . . Hence when she is being preached and venerated, she summons the faithful to her Son and his sacrifice, and to love for the Father."[64] For this reason, Mary's faith, according to the Church's apostolic witness, in some way continues to become the faith of the pilgrim People of God: the faith of individuals and

[64] Ibid., 65.

communities, of places and gatherings, and of the various groups existing in the Church. It is a faith that is passed on simultaneously through both the mind and the heart. It is gained or regained continually through prayer. Therefore, *"the Church* in her apostolic work also *rightly looks to her who brought forth Christ*, conceived by the Holy Spirit and born of the Virgin, so that through the Church Christ *may be born and increase in the hearts of the faithful also*."[65]

Today, as on this pilgrimage of faith we draw near to the end of the second Christian Millennium, the Church, through the teaching of the Second Vatican Council, calls our attention to her vision of herself, as the "one People of God . . . among all the nations of the earth". And she reminds us of that truth according to which all the faithful, though "scattered throughout the world are in communion with each other in the Holy Spirit".[66] We can therefore say that in this union the mystery of Pentecost is continually being accomplished. At the same time, the Lord's apostles and disciples, in all the nations of the earth, "devote themselves to prayer *together with Mary, the mother of Jesus*" (Acts 1:14). As they constitute from generation to generation the "sign of the kingdom" which is not of

[65] Ibid., 65.
[66] Cf. ibid., 13.

this world,[67] they are also aware that in the midst of this world they must *gather around that King* to whom the nations have been given in heritage (cf. Ps 2:8), to whom the Father has given "the throne of David his father", so that he "will reign over the house of Jacob forever, and of his kingdom there will be no end".

During this time of vigil, Mary, through the same faith which made her blessed, especially from the moment of the Annunciation, is *present* in the Church's mission, *present* in the Church's work of introducing into the world *the kingdom of her Son*.[68]

This presence of Mary finds many different expressions in our day just as it did throughout the Church's history. It also has a wide field of action: through the faith and piety of individual believers; through the traditions of Christian families or "domestic churches", of parish and missionary communities, religious institutes and dioceses; through the radiance and attraction of the great shrines where not only individuals or local groups, but sometimes whole nations and societies, even whole continents, seek to meet the Mother of the Lord, the one who is blessed because she believed, is the first among believers and therefore became

[67] Cf. ibid., 13.
[68] Cf. ibid., 13.

the Mother of Emmanuel. This is the message of
the Land of Palestine, the spiritual homeland of all
Christians because it was the homeland of the
Savior of the world and of his Mother. This is
the message of the many churches in Rome and
throughout the world which have been raised up
in the course of the centuries by the faith of
Christians. This is the message of centers like
Guadalupe, Lourdes, Fatima, and the others situated in the various countries. Among them how
could I fail to mention the one in my own native
land, Jasna Góra? One could perhaps speak of a
specific "geography" of faith and Marian devotion, which includes all these special places of
pilgrimage where the People of God seek to meet
the Mother of God in order to find, within the
radius of the maternal presence of her "who
believed", a strengthening of their own faith. For
in Mary's faith, first at the Annunciation and then
fully at the foot of the Cross, an *interior space* was
reopened within humanity which the eternal Father
can fill "with every spiritual blessing". It is the
space "of the new and eternal Covenant",[69] and it
continues to exist in the Church, which in Christ
is "a kind of sacrament or sign of intimate union
with God, and of the unity of all mankind".[70]

[69] Cf. Roman Missal, formula of the Consecration of the
Chalice in the Eucharistic Prayers.

[70] *Lumen Gentium*, 1.

In the faith which Mary professed at the Annunciation as the "handmaid of the Lord" and in which she constantly "precedes" the pilgrim People of God throughout the earth, the *Church* "*strives* energetically and constantly *to bring* all *humanity . . . back to Christ its Head* in the unity of his Spirit".[71]

2. *The Church's journey and the unity of all Christians*

29. "In all of Christ's disciples the Spirit arouses the desire to be peacefully *united*, in the manner determined by Christ, as one flock *under one shepherd*."[72] The journey of the Church, especially in our own time, is marked by the sign of ecumenism: Christians are seeking ways to restore that unity which Christ implored from the Father for his disciples on the day before his Passion: "*That they may all be one*; even as you, Father, are in me, and I in you, that they also may be in us, so that the world *may believe* that you have sent me" (Jn 17:21). The unity of Christ's disciples, therefore, is a great sign given in order to kindle faith in the world, while their division constitutes a scandal.[73]

[71] Ibid., 13
[72] Ibid., 15.
[73] Cf. Second Vatican Ecumenical Council, Decree on

The ecumenical movement, on the basis of a clearer and more widespread awareness of the urgent need to achieve the unity of all Christians, has found on the part of the Catholic Church its culminating expression in the work of the Second Vatican Council: Christians must deepen in themselves and each of their communities that "obedience of faith" of which Mary is the first and brightest example. And since she "shines forth on earth, . . . as a sign of sure hope and solace for the pilgrim People of God", "it gives great joy and comfort to this most holy Synod that *among the divided brethren*, too, there are those who give due honor to the Mother of our Lord and Savior. This is especially so among the Easterners."[74]

30. Christians know that their unity will be truly rediscovered only if it is based on the unity of their faith. They must resolve considerable discrepancies of doctrine concerning the mystery and ministry of the Church, and sometimes also concerning the role of Mary in the work of salvation.[75] The dialogues begun by the Catholic Church with the

Ecumenism *Unitatis Redintegratio*, 1.

[74] *Lumen Gentium*, 68, 69. On Mary Most Holy, promoter of Christian unity, and on devotion to Mary in the East, cf. Leo XIII, Encyclical Epistle *Adjutricem Populi*, (September 5, 1895): *Acta Leonis*, XV, 300–312.

[75] Cf. *Unitatis Redintegratio*, 20.

churches and ecclesial communities of the West[76] are steadily converging upon these *two inseparable aspects* of the same mystery of salvation. If the mystery of the Word made flesh enables us to glimpse the mystery of the divine motherhood and if, in turn, contemplation of the Mother of God brings us to a more profound understanding of the mystery of the Incarnation, then the same must be said for the mystery of the Church and Mary's role in the work of salvation. By a more profound study of both Mary and the Church, clarifying each by the light of the other, Christians who are eager to do what Jesus tells them—as their Mother recommends (cf. Jn 2:5)—will be able to go forward together on this "pilgrimage of faith". Mary, who is still the model of this pilgrimage, is to lead them to the unity which is willed by their one Lord and so much desired by those who are attentively listening to what "the Spirit is saying to the churches" today (Rev 2:7, 11, 17).

Meanwhile, it is a hopeful sign that these churches and ecclesial communities are finding agreement with the Catholic Church on fundamental points of Christian belief, including matters relating to the Virgin Mary. For they recognize her as the Mother of the Lord and hold that this forms part of our faith in Christ, true God and true man.

[76] Cf. ibid., 19.

They look to her who at the foot of the Cross accepts as her son the beloved disciple, the one who in his turn accepts her as his mother.

Therefore, why should we not all together look to her as *our common Mother*, who prays for the unity of God's family and who "precedes" us all at the head of the long line of witnesses of faith in the one Lord, the Son of God, who was conceived in her virginal womb by the power of the Holy Spirit?

31. On the other hand, I wish to emphasize how profoundly the Catholic Church, the Orthodox Church and the ancient churches of the East feel united by love and praise of the *Theotókos*. Not only "basic dogmas of the Christian Faith concerning the Trinity and God's Word made flesh of the Virgin Mary were defined in Ecumenical Councils held in the East",[77] but also in their liturgical worship "the Orientals pay high tribute, in very beautiful hymns, to Mary ever Virgin . . . God's Most Holy Mother".[78]

The brethren of these churches have experienced a complex history, but it is one that has always been marked by an intense desire for Christian commitment and apostolic activity, despite fre-

[77] Ibid., 14.
[78] Ibid., 15.

quent persecution, even to the point of bloodshed. It is a history of fidelity to the Lord, an authentic "pilgrimage of faith" in space and time, during which Eastern Christians have always looked with boundless trust to the Mother of the Lord, celebrated her with praise and invoked her with unceasing prayer. In the difficult moments of their troubled Christian existence "they have taken refuge under her protection",[79] conscious of having in her a powerful aid. The churches which profess the doctrine of Ephesus proclaim the Virgin as "true Mother of God" since "Our Lord Jesus Christ, born of the Father before time began according to his divinity, in the last days he himself, for our sake and for our salvation, was begotten of Mary the Virgin Mother of God according to his humanity."[80] The Greek Fathers and the Byzantine tradition, contemplating the Virgin in the light of the Word made flesh, have sought to penetrate the depth of that bond which unites Mary, as the Mother of God, to Christ, and the Church: the Virgin is a permanent presence in the whole reality of the salvific mystery.

The Coptic and Ethiopian traditions were introduced to this contemplation of the mystery of Mary by Saint Cyril of Alexandria, and in their

[79] *Lumen Gentium*, 66.

[80] Ecumenical Council of Chalcedon, *Definitio fidei*: *Conciliorum Oecumenicorum Decreta*, Bologna 1973, 86 (*DS* 301).

turn they have celebrated it with a profuse poetic blossoming.[81] The poetic genius of Saint Ephrem the Syrian, called "the lyre of the Holy Spirit", tirelessly sang of Mary, leaving a still living mark on the whole tradition of the Syriac Church.[82]

In his panegyric of the *Theotókos*, Saint Gregory of Narek, one of the outstanding glories of Armenia, with powerful poetic inspiration ponders the different aspects of the mystery of the Incarnation, and each of them is for him an occasion to sing and extol the extraordinary dignity and magnificent beauty of the Virgin Mary, Mother of the Word made flesh.[83]

It does not surprise us therefore that Mary occupies a privileged place in the worship of the ancient Oriental churches with an incomparable abundance of feasts and hymns.

32. In the Byzantine liturgy, in all the hours of the Divine Office, praise of the Mother is linked

[81] Cf. The *Weddâsê Mâryâm* [Praises of Mary] which follows the Ethiopian Psalter and contains hymns and prayers to Mary for each day of the week. Cf. also the *Matshafa Kidâna Mehrat* [Book of the Pact of Mercy]; the importance given to Mary in the Ethiopian hymnology and liturgy deserves to be emphasized.

[82] Cf. Saint Ephrem, *Hymn. de Nativitate: Scriptores Syri*, 82, *CSCO*, 186.

[83] Cf. Saint Gregory of Narek, *Le livre de prières: S. Ch.* 78, 160–63; 428–32.

with praise of her Son and with the praise which, through the Son, is offered up to the Father in the Holy Spirit. In the *Anaphora* or Eucharistic Prayer of Saint John Chrysostom, immediately after the *epiclesis* the assembled community sings in honor of the Mother of God: "It is truly just to proclaim you blessed, O Mother of God, who are most blessed, all pure and Mother of our God. We magnify you who are more honorable than the Cherubim and incomparably more glorious than the Seraphim. You who, without losing your virginity, gave birth to the Word of God. You who are truly the Mother of God."

These praises, which in every celebration of the Eucharistic Liturgy are offered to Mary, have molded the faith, piety, and prayer of the faithful. In the course of the centuries they have permeated their whole spiritual outlook, fostering in them a profound devotion to the "All Holy Mother of God".

33. This year there occurs the twelfth centenary of the Second Ecumenical Council of Nicaea (787). Putting an end to the well known controversy about the cult of sacred images, this Council defined that, according to the teaching of the holy Fathers and the universal Tradition of the Church, there could be exposed for the veneration of the faithful, together with the Cross, also images of

the Mother of God, of the angels and of the saints, in churches and houses and at the roadside.[84] This custom has been maintained in the whole of the East and also in the West. Images of the Virgin have a place of honor in churches and houses. In them Mary is represented in a number of ways: as the throne of God carrying the Lord and giving him to humanity (*Theotókos*); as the way that leads to Christ and manifests him (*Hodegetria*); as a praying figure in an attitude of intercession and as a sign of the divine presence on the journey of the faithful until the day of the Lord (*Deësis*); as the protectress who stretches out her mantle over the peoples (*Pokrov*); or as the merciful Virgin of tenderness (*Eleousa*). She is usually represented with her Son, the child Jesus, in her arms: it is the relationship with the Son which glorifies the Mother. Sometimes she embraces him with tenderness (*Glykophilousa*); at other times she is a hieratic figure, apparently rapt in contemplation of him who is the Lord of history (cf. Rev 5:9–14).[85]

It is also appropriate to mention the icon of Our Lady of Vladimir, which continually accompanied the pilgrimage of faith of the peoples of the ancient Rus'. The first Millennium of the conversion of those noble lands to Christianity is approaching: lands of humble folk, of thinkers and of saints.

[84] Second Ecumenical Council of Nicaea: *Conciliorum Oecumenicorum Decreta*, Bologna 1973, 135–38 (*DS* 600–609).

[85] Cf. *Lumen Gentium*, 59.

The icons are still venerated in the Ukraine, in Byelorussia and in Russia under various titles. They are images which witness to the faith and spirit of prayer of that people, who sense the presence and protection of the Mother of God. In these icons the Virgin shines as the image of divine beauty, the abode of Eternal Wisdom, the figure of the one who prays, the prototype of contemplation, the image of glory: she who even in her earthly life possessed the spiritual knowledge inaccessible to human reasoning and who attained through faith the most sublime knowledge. I also recall the icon of the Virgin of the Cenacle, praying with the Apostles as they awaited the Holy Spirit: could she not become the sign of hope for all those who, in fraternal dialogue, wish to deepen their obedience of faith?

34. Such a wealth of praise, built up by the different forms of the Church's great Tradition, could help us to hasten the day when the Church can begin once more to breathe fully with her "two lungs", the East and the West. As I have often said, this is more than ever necessary today. It would be an effective aid in furthering the progress of the dialogue already taking place between the Catholic Church and the churches and ecclesial communities of the West.[86] It would also be the

[86] Cf. *Unitatis Redintegratio*, 19.

way for the pilgrim Church to sing and to live more perfectly her "*Magnificat*".

3. The "Magnificat" of the pilgrim Church

35. At the present stage of her journey, therefore, the Church seeks to rediscover the unity of all who profess their faith in Christ, in order to show obedience to her Lord, who prayed for this unity before his Passion. "Like a pilgrim in a foreign land, the Church presses forward amid the persecutions of the world and the consolations of God, announcing the Cross and Death of the Lord until he comes."[87] "Moving forward through trial and tribulation, *the Church is strengthened by the power of God's grace promised to her by the Lord*, so that in the weakness of the flesh she may not waver from perfect fidelity, but remain a bride worthy of her Lord; that moved by the Holy Spirit she may never cease to renew herself, until through the Cross she arrives at the light which knows no setting."[88]

The Virgin Mother is constantly present on this journey of faith of the People of God toward the light. This is shown in a special way by *the canticle of the "Magnificat", which, having welled up from the depths of Mary's faith* at the Visitation, ceaselessly

[87] *Lumen Gentium*, 8.
[88] Ibid., 9.

re-echoes in the heart of the Church down the centuries. This is proved by its daily recitation in the liturgy of Vespers and at many other moments of both personal and communal devotion.

"My soul magnifies the Lord,
and my spirit rejoices in God my Savior,
for he has looked on his servant in her lowliness.
For behold, henceforth all generations will call me
    blessed;
for he who is mighty has done great things for me,
and holy is his name;
And his mercy is from age to age
on those who fear him.
He has shown strength with his arm,
he has scattered the proud-hearted,
he has cast down the mighty from their thrones,
and lifted up the lowly;
he has filled the hungry with good things,
sent the rich away empty.
He has helped his servant Israel,
remembering his mercy,
as he spoke to our fathers,
to Abraham and to his posterity forever."

                          (Lk 1:46–55)

36. When Elizabeth greeted her young kins-woman coming from Nazareth, *Mary replied with the Magnificat*. In her greeting, Elizabeth first called Mary "blessed" because of "the fruit

of her womb", and then she called her "blessed" because of her faith (cf. Lk 1:42, 45). These two blessings referred directly to the Annunciation. Now, at the Visitation, when Elizabeth's greeting bears witness to that culminating moment, Mary's faith acquires a new consciousness and a new expression. That which remained hidden in the depths of the "obedience of faith" at the Annunciation can now be said to spring forth like a clear and life-giving flame of the spirit. The words used by Mary on the threshold of Elizabeth's house are *an inspired profession of her faith*, in which *her response to the revealed word* is expressed with the religious and poetical exultation of her whole being toward God. In these sublime words, which are simultaneously very simple and wholly inspired by the sacred texts of the people of Israel,[89] Mary's personal experience, the ecstasy of her heart, shines forth. In them shines a ray of the mystery of God, the glory of his ineffable holiness, the eternal *love which, as an irrevocable gift, enters into human history*.

Mary is the first to share in this new revelation of God and, within the same, in this new "self-giving" of God. Therefore she proclaims: "For he who is mighty has done great things for me, and holy is his name." Her words reflect a joy of spirit

[89] As is well known, the words of the *Magnificat* contain or echo numerous passages of the Old Testament.

which is difficult to express: "My spirit rejoices in God my Savior." Indeed, "the deepest truth about God and the salvation of man is made clear to us in Christ, who is at the same time the mediator and the fullness of all revelation."[90] In her exultation Mary confesses that she finds herself *in the very heart of this fullness* of Christ. She is conscious that the promise made to the fathers, first of all "to Abraham and to his posterity forever", is being fulfilled in herself. She is thus aware that concentrated within herself as the Mother of Christ is *the whole salvific economy*, in which "from age to age" is manifested he who, as the God of the Covenant, "remembers his mercy".

37. The Church, which from the beginning has modeled her earthly journey on that of the Mother of God, constantly repeats after her the words of the *Magnificat*. From the depths of the Virgin's faith at the Annunciation and the Visitation, the Church derives the truth about the God of the Covenant: the God who is Almighty and does "great things" for man: "holy is his name". In the *Magnificat* the Church sees uprooted that sin which is found at the outset of the earthly history of man and woman, the sin of disbelief and of "little faith" in God. In contrast with the "suspicion"

[90] *Dei Verbum*, 2.

which the "father of lies" sowed in the heart of
Eve the first woman, Mary, whom tradition is
wont to call the "new Eve"[91] and the true "Mother
of the living",[92] boldly proclaims the *undimmed*
truth about God: the holy and almighty God, who
from the beginning is *the source of all gifts*, he who
"has done great things" in her, as well as in the
whole universe. In the act of creation God gives
existence to all that is. In creating man, God gives
him the dignity of the image and likeness of himself in a special way as compared with all earthly
creatures. Moreover, in his desire to give, *God
gives himself in the Son*, notwithstanding man's sin:
"He so loved the world that he gave his only Son"
(Jn 3:16). Mary is the first witness of this marvelous
truth, which will be fully accomplished through
"the works and words" (cf. Acts 1:1) of her Son and
definitively through his Cross and Resurrection.

The Church, which even "amid trials and tribu-
lations" does not cease repeating with Mary the
words of the *Magnificat*, is sustained by the power
of God's truth, proclaimed on that occasion with
such extraordinary simplicity. At the same time,

[91] Cf. for example Saint Justin, *Dialogus cum Tryphone
Iudaeo*, 100: Otto II, 358; Saint Irenaeus, *Adversus Haereses* III,
22, 4: *S. Ch.* 211, 439–45; Tertullian, *De carne Christi*, 17, 4–6:
CCL 2, 904f.

[92] Cf. Saint Epiphanius, *Panarion*, III 2: *Haer.* 78, 18:
PG 42, 727–30.

by means of this truth about God the Church *desires to shed light upon* the difficult and sometimes tangled paths of man's earthly existence. The Church's journey, therefore, near the end of the second Christian Millennium, involves a renewed commitment to her mission. Following him who said of himself: "(God) has anointed me *to preach good news to the poor*" (cf. Lk 4:18), the Church has sought from generation to generation and still seeks today to accomplish that same mission.

The Church's *love of preference for the poor* is wonderfully inscribed in Mary's *Magnificat*. The God of the Covenant, celebrated in the exultation of her spirit by the Virgin of Nazareth, is also he who "has cast down the mighty from their thrones, and lifted up the lowly, . . . filled the hungry with good things, sent the rich away empty, . . . scattered the proud-hearted . . . and his mercy is from age to age on those who fear him". Mary is deeply imbued with the spirit of the "poor of Yahweh", who in the prayer of the Psalms awaited from God their salvation, placing all their trust in him (cf. Ps 25; 31; 35; 55). Mary truly proclaims the coming of the "Messiah of the poor" (cf. Is 11:4; 61:1). Drawing from Mary's heart, from the depth of her faith expressed in the words of the *Magnificat*, the Church renews ever more effectively in herself the awareness that *the truth about God who saves*, the truth about God who is the source of every gift, *cannot be separated from the manifestation of his love of preference for the poor and humble*, that love which, celebrated in the *Magnificat*, is later expressed in the words and works of Jesus.

The Church is thus aware—and at the present time this awareness is particularly vivid—not only that these two elements of the message contained in the *Magnificat* cannot be separated, but also that there is a duty to safeguard carefully the importance of "the poor" and of "the option in favor of the poor" in the word of the living God. These are matters and questions intimately connected with the *Christian meaning of freedom and liberation*. "Mary is totally dependent upon God and completely directed toward him, and, at the side of her Son, she is *the most perfect image of freedom and of the liberation* of humanity and of the universe. It is to her as Mother and Model that the Church must look in order to understand in its completeness the meaning of her own mission."[93]

[93] Congregation for the Doctrine of the Faith, *Instruction on Christian Freedom and Liberation* (March 22, 1986), 97.

CHAPTER THREE

MATERNAL MEDIATION

1. *Mary, the Handmaid of the Lord*

38. The Church knows and teaches with Saint Paul that *there is only one mediator*: "For there is one God, and there is one mediator between God and men, the man Christ Jesus, who gave himself as a ransom for all" (1 Tim 2:5–6). "The maternal role of Mary toward people in no way obscures or diminishes the unique mediation of Christ, but rather shows its power":[94] it is mediation in Christ.

The Church knows and teaches that "all *the saving influences of the Blessed Virgin* on mankind originate . . . from the divine pleasure. They flow forth *from the superabundance of the merits of Christ*, rest on his mediation, depend entirely on it, and draw all their power from it. In no way do they impede the immediate union of the faithful with Christ. Rather, they foster this union."[95] This saving influence is sustained by the Holy Spirit,

[94] *Lumen Gentium*, 60.
[95] Ibid., 60.

who, just as he overshadowed the Virgin Mary when he began in her the divine motherhood, in a similar way constantly sustains her solicitude for the brothers and sisters of her Son.

In effect, Mary's mediation *is intimately linked with her motherhood*. It possesses a specifically maternal character, which distinguishes it from the mediation of the other creatures who in various and always subordinate ways share in the one mediation of Christ, although her own mediation is also a shared mediation.[96] In fact, while it is true that "no creature could ever be classed with the Incarnate Word and Redeemer", at the same time "the unique mediation of the Redeemer does not exclude but rather gives rise among creatures to *a manifold cooperation* which is but a sharing in this unique source". And thus "the one goodness of God is in reality communicated diversely to his creatures".[97]

The teaching of the Second Vatican Council presents the truth of Mary's mediation as "a *sharing in the one unique source that is the mediation of Christ himself*". Thus we read: "The Church does not

[96] Cf. the formula of mediatrix "ad Mediatorem" of Saint Bernard, *In Dominica infra oct. Assumptionis Sermo*, 2: *S. Bernardi Opera*, V, 1968, 263. Mary as a pure mirror sends back to her Son all the glory and honor which she receives. Id., *In Nativitate B. Mariae Sermo—De Aquaeductu*, 12: ed. cit., 283.

[97] *Lumen Gentium*, 62.

hesitate to profess this subordinate role of Mary. She experiences it continuously and commends it to the hearts of the faithful, so that encouraged by this maternal help they may more closely adhere to the Mediator and Redeemer."[98] This role is at the same time *special and extraordinary*. It flows from her divine motherhood and can be understood and lived in faith only on the basis of the full truth of this motherhood. Since by virtue of divine election Mary is the earthly Mother of the Father's consubstantial Son and his "generous companion" in the work of redemption, "she is a mother to us in the order of grace".[99] This role constitutes a real dimension of her presence in the saving mystery of Christ and the Church.

39. From this point of view we must consider once more the fundamental event in the economy of salvation, namely the Incarnation of the Word at the moment of the Annunciation. It is significant that Mary, recognizing in the words of the divine messenger the will of the Most High and submitting to his power, says: *"Behold, I am the handmaid* of the Lord; let it be to me according to your word"* (Lk 1:38). The first moment of submission to the one mediation "between God and

[98] Ibid., 62.
[99] Ibid., 61.

men"—the mediation of Jesus Christ—is the Virgin of Nazareth's acceptance of motherhood. Mary consents to God's choice, in order to become through the power of the Holy Spirit the Mother of the Son of God. It can be said that this *consent to motherhood* is above all *a result of her total self-giving to God in virginity*. Mary accepted her election as Mother of the Son of God, guided by spousal love, the love which totally "consecrates" a human being to God. By virtue of this love, Mary wished to be always and in all things "given to God", living in virginity. The words "Behold, I am the handmaid of the Lord" express the fact that from the outset she accepted and understood her own motherhood as a total *gift of self*, a gift of her person to the service of the saving plans of the Most High. And to the very end she lived her entire maternal sharing in the life of Jesus Christ, her Son, in a way that matched her vocation to virginity. Mary's motherhood, completely pervaded by her spousal attitude as the "handmaid of the Lord", constitutes the first and fundamental dimension of that mediation which the Church confesses and proclaims in her regard[100] and continually "commends to the hearts of the faithful", since the Church has great trust in her. For it must be recognized that before anyone else it was God

[100] Ibid., 62.

himself, the Eternal Father, who *entrusted himself to the Virgin of Nazareth*, giving her his own Son in the mystery of the Incarnation. Her election to the supreme office and dignity of Mother of the Son of God refers, on the ontological level, to the very reality of the union of the two natures in the person of the Word (*hypostatic union*). This basic fact of being the Mother of the Son of God is from the very beginning a complete openness to the person of Christ, to his whole work, to his whole mission. The words "Behold, I am the handmaid of the Lord" testify to Mary's openness of spirit: she perfectly unites in herself the love proper to virginity and the love characteristic of motherhood, which are joined and as it were fused together.

For this reason Mary became not only the "nursing mother" of the Son of Man but also the "associate of unique nobility"[101] of the Messiah and Redeemer. As I have already said, she advanced in her pilgrimage of faith, and in this *pilgrimage* to the foot of the Cross there was simultaneously accomplished her maternal *cooperation* with the Savior's whole mission through her actions and sufferings. Along the path of this collaboration with the work of her Son, the Redeemer, Mary's motherhood itself underwent a singular transformation, becoming ever more imbued with "burning

[101] Ibid., 61.

charity" toward all those to whom Christ's mission was directed. Through this "burning charity", which sought to achieve, in union with Christ, the restoration of "supernatural life to souls",[102] Mary *entered, in a way all her own, into the one mediation* "between God and men" *which is the mediation of the man Christ Jesus*. If she was the first to experience within herself the supernatural consequences of this one mediation—in the Annunciation she had been greeted as "full of grace"—then we must say that through this fullness of grace and supernatural life she was especially predisposed to cooperation with Christ, the one Mediator of human salvation. *And such cooperation* is *precisely this mediation subordinated* to the mediation of Christ.

In Mary's case we have a special and exceptional mediation, based upon her "fullness of grace", which was expressed in the complete willingness of the "handmaid of the Lord". In response to this interior willingness of his Mother, *Jesus Christ prepared her* ever more completely to become for all people their "mother in the order of grace". This is indicated, at least indirectly, by certain details noted by the Synoptics (cf. Lk 11:28; 8:20–21; Mk 3:32–35; Mt 12:47–50) and still more so by the Gospel of John (cf. 2:1–12; 19:25–27), which I have already mentioned. Particularly elo-

[102] Ibid., 61.

quent in this regard are the words spoken by Jesus on the Cross to Mary and John.

40. After the events of the Resurrection and Ascension, Mary entered the Upper Room together with the Apostles to await Pentecost, and was present there as the Mother of the glorified Lord. She was not only the one who "advanced in her pilgrimage of faith" and loyally persevered in her union with her Son "unto the Cross", *but she was also the "handmaid of the Lord", left by her Son as Mother in the midst of the infant Church*: "Behold your mother." Thus there began to develop a special bond between this Mother and the Church. For the infant Church was the fruit of the Cross and Resurrection of her Son. Mary, who from the beginning had given herself without reserve to the person and work of her Son, could not but pour out upon the Church, from the very beginning, her maternal self-giving. After her Son's departure, her motherhood remains in the Church as maternal mediation: interceding for all her children, the Mother cooperates in the saving work of her Son, the Redeemer of the world. In fact the Council teaches that the "motherhood of Mary in the order of grace . . . *will last without interruption* until the eternal fulfillment of all the elect".[103] With the re-

[103] Ibid., 62.

deeming death of her Son, the maternal mediation of the handmaid of the Lord took on a universal dimension, for the work of redemption embraces the whole of humanity. Thus there is manifested in a singular way the efficacy of the one and universal mediation of Christ "between God and men". Mary's cooperation shares, in its subordinate character, *in the universality of the mediation of the Redeemer*, the one Mediator. This is clearly indicated by the Council in the words quoted above.

"For," the text goes on, "taken up to heaven, she did not lay aside this saving role, but by her manifold acts of intercession continues to win for us gifts of eternal salvation".[104] With this character of "intercession", first manifested at Cana in Galilee, Mary's mediation continues in the history of the Church and the world. We read that Mary "by her maternal charity, cares for the brethren of her Son who still journey on earth surrounded by dangers and difficulties, until they are led to their happy homeland".[105] In this way

[104] Ibid., 62.

[105] Ibid., 62; in her prayer too the Church recognizes and celebrates Mary's "maternal role"; it is a role "of intercession and forgiveness, petition and grace, reconciliation and peace" (cf. Preface of the Mass of the Blessed Virgin Mary, Mother and Mediatrix of Grace, in *Collectio Missarum de Beata Maria Virgine*, ed. typ., 1987, I, 120).

Mary's motherhood continues unceasingly in the Church as the mediation which intercedes, and the Church expresses her faith in this truth by invoking Mary "under the titles of Advocate, Auxiliatrix, Adjutrix and Mediatrix".[106]

41. Through her mediation, subordinate to that of the Redeemer, Mary contributes *in a special way to the union of the pilgrim Church* on earth with the eschatological and heavenly *reality* of the communion of saints, since she has already been "assumed into heaven".[107] The truth of the Assumption, defined by Pius XII, is reaffirmed by the Second Vatican Council, which thus expresses the Church's faith: "Preserved free from all guilt of original sin, the Immaculate Virgin *was taken up body and soul into heavenly glory* upon the completion of her earthly sojourn. She was *exalted* by the Lord *as Queen of the Universe*, in order that she might be the more thoroughly conformed to her Son, the Lord of lords (cf. Rev 19:16) and the conqueror of sin and death."[108] In this teaching Pius XII was in

[106] Ibid., 62

[107] Ibid., 62; cf. Saint John Damascene, *Hom. in Dormitionem*, I, 11; II, 2, 14; III, 2: *S. Ch.* 80, 111f.; 127–31; 157–61; 181–85; Saint Bernard, *In Assumptione Beatae Mariae Sermo*, 1–2: *S. Bernardi Opera*, V, 1968, 228–38.

[108] *Lumen Gentium*, 59; cf. Pope Pius XII, Apostolic Constitution *Munificentissimus Deus* (November 1, 1950):

continuity with Tradition, which has found many different expressions in the history of the Church, both in the East and in the West.

By the mystery of the Assumption into heaven there were definitively accomplished in Mary all the effects of the one mediation of *Christ the Redeemer of the world* and *Risen Lord*: "In Christ shall all be made alive. But each in his own order: Christ the first fruits, then at his coming those who belong to Christ" (1 Cor 15:22–23). In the mystery of the Assumption is expressed the faith of the Church, according to which Mary is "united by a close and indissoluble bond" to Christ, for, if as Virgin and Mother she was singularly united with him *in his first coming*, so through her continued collaboration with him she will be united with him in expectation of the second; "redeemed in an especially sublime manner by reason of the merits of her Son",[109] she also has that specifically maternal role of mediatrix of mercy *at his final coming*, when all those who belong to Christ "shall be made alive", when "the last enemy to be destroyed is death" (1 Cor 15:26).[110]

AAS 42 (1950) 769–71; Saint Bernard presents Mary immersed in the splendor of the Son's glory: *In Dominica infra oct. Assumptionis Sermo*, 3; *S. Bernardi Opera*, V, 1968, 263f.

[109] *Lumen Gentium*, 53.

[110] On this particular aspect of Mary's mediation as *implorer of clemency* from the "Son as Judge", cf. Saint Bernard, *In*

Connected with this exaltation of the noble "Daughter of Zion"[111] through her Assumption into heaven is the mystery of her eternal glory. For the Mother of Christ is glorified as "Queen of the Universe".[112] She who at the Annunciation called herself the "handmaid of the Lord" remained throughout her earthly life faithful to what this name expresses. In this she confirmed that she was a true "disciple" of Christ, who strongly emphasized that his mission was one of service: the Son of Man "came not to be served but to serve, and to give his life as a ransom for many" (Mt 20:28). In this way Mary became the first of those who "serving Christ also in others with humility and patience lead their brothers and sisters to that King whom to serve is to reign",[113] and she fully obtained that "state of royal freedom" proper to Christ's disciples: to serve means to reign!

"Christ obeyed even at the cost of death, and was therefore raised up by the Father (cf. Phil 2:8–9). Thus he entered into the glory of his kingdom. To him all things are made subject until he subjects himself and all created things to the Father, that

---

Dominica infra oct. Assumptionis Sermo, 1–2: *S. Bernardi Opera*, V, 1968, 262f.; Pope Leo XIII, Encyclical Epistle *Octobri Mense* (September 22, 1891): *Acta Leonis*, XI, 299–315.

[111] *Lumen Gentium*, 55.
[112] Ibid., 59.
[113] Ibid., 36.

God may be all in all (cf. 1 Cor 15:27–28)."[114]
Mary, the handmaid of the Lord, has a share in
this kingdom of the Son.[115] The *glory of serving*
does not cease to be her royal exaltation: assumed
into heaven, she does not cease her saving service,
which expresses her maternal mediation "until the
eternal fulfillment of all the elect".[116] Thus, she
who here on earth "loyally persevered in her union
with her Son unto the Cross", continues to remain
united with him, while now *"all things are subjected
to him, until he subjects to the Father himself and all
things"*. Thus in her Assumption into heaven,
Mary is as it were clothed by the whole reality of
the communion of saints, and her very union with
the Son in glory is wholly oriented toward the
definitive fullness of the kingdom, *when "God will
be all in all"*.

In this phase too Mary's maternal mediation does
not cease to be subordinate to him who is the one
Mediator, *until the final realization of "the fullness of
time"*, that is to say until "all things are united in
Christ" (cf. Eph 1:10).

[114] Ibid., 36.

[115] With regard to Mary as Queen, cf. Saint John Damascene,
Hom. in Nativitatem, 6; 12; *Hom. in Dormitionem*, I, 2, 12, 14;
II, 11; III, 4: *S. Ch.* 80, 59f.; 83f.; 113f.; 117; 151f.; 189–93.

[116] *Lumen Gentium*, 62.

2. *Mary in the life of the Church and of every Christian*

42. Linking itself with Tradition, the Second Vatican Council brought new light to bear on the role of the Mother of Christ in the life of the Church. "Through the gift . . . of divine motherhood, Mary is united with her Son, the Redeemer, and with his singular graces and offices. By these, the Blessed Virgin is also intimately united with the Church: *the Mother of God is a figure of the Church* in the matter of faith, charity, and perfect union with Christ."[117] We have already noted how, from the beginning, Mary remains with the Apostles in expectation of Pentecost and how, as "the blessed one who believed", she is present in the midst of the pilgrim Church from generation to generation through faith and as the model of the hope which does not disappoint (cf. Rom 5:5).

Mary believed in the fulfillment of what had been said to her by the Lord. As Virgin, she believed that she would conceive and bear a son: the "Holy One", who bears the name of "Son of God", the name "Jesus" (= God who saves). As handmaid of the Lord, she remained in perfect fidelity to the person and mission of this Son. As Mother, "*believing and obeying* . . . she brought forth on earth *the Father's Son*. This she did,

[117] Ibid., 63.

knowing not man but overshadowed by the Holy Spirit."[118]

For these reasons Mary is honored in the Church "with special reverence. Indeed, from most ancient times the Blessed Virgin Mary has been venerated under the title of 'God-bearer'. In all perils and needs, the faithful have fled prayerfully to her protection."[119] This cult is altogether special: it bears in itself and *expresses* the profound *link* which exists *between the Mother of Christ and the Church*.[120] As Virgin and Mother, Mary remains for the Church a "permanent model". It can therefore be said that especially under this aspect, namely as a model, or rather as a "figure", Mary, present in the mystery of Christ, remains constantly present also in the mystery of the Church. For the Church too is "called mother and virgin", and these names have a profound biblical and theological justification.[121]

43. The *Church* "*becomes* herself *a mother* by accepting God's word with fidelity".[122] Like Mary

---

[118] Ibid., 63.

[119] Ibid., 66.

[120] Cf. Saint Ambrose, *De Institutione Virginis*, XIV, 88–89: *PL* 16, 341; Saint Augustine, *Sermo* 215, 4: *PL* 38, 1074; *De Sancta Virginitate*, II, 2; V, 5; VI, 6: *PL* 40, 397; 398f.; 399; *Sermo* 191, II, 3: *PL* 38, 1010f.

[121] *Lumen Gentium*, 63.

[122] Ibid., 64.

who first believed by accepting the word of God revealed to her at the Annunciation and by remaining faithful to that word in all her trials even unto the Cross, so too the Church becomes a mother when, *accepting with fidelity the word of God*, "by her preaching and by baptism *she brings forth to a new and immortal life children* who are conceived *of the Holy Spirit* and born of God".[123] This "maternal" characteristic of the Church was expressed in a particularly vivid way by the Apostle to the Gentiles when he wrote: "My little children, with whom I am again in travail until Christ be formed in you!" (Gal 4:19). These words of Saint Paul contain an interesting sign of the early Church's awareness of her own motherhood, linked to her apostolic service to mankind. This awareness enabled and still enables the Church to see the mystery of her life and mission modeled *upon the example of the Mother of the Son*, who is "the first-born among many brethren" (Rom 8:29).

It can be said that from Mary the Church also learns her own motherhood: she recognizes the maternal dimension of her vocation, which is essentially bound to her sacramental nature, in "contemplating Mary's mysterious sanctity, imitating her charity, and faithfully fulfilling the Father's will".[124] If the Church is the sign and instrument

[123] Ibid., 64.
[124] Ibid., 64.

of intimate union with God, she is so by reason of
her motherhood, because, receiving life from the
Spirit, she "generates" sons and daughters of the
human race to a new life in Christ. For just as *Mary
is at the service of the mystery of the Incarnation*, so *the
Church* is always *at the service of the mystery of
adoption to sonship* through grace.

Likewise, following the example of Mary,
the Church remains the virgin faithful to her
spouse: "The Church herself is a virgin, who
keeps whole and pure the fidelity she has pledged
to her Spouse."[125] For the Church is the spouse of
Christ, as is clear from the Pauline Letters (cf.
Eph 5:21–33; 2 Cor 11:2), and from the title found
in John: "bride of the Lamb" (Rev 21:9). If *the
Church* as spouse "keeps the fidelity she *has pledged*
to Christ", this fidelity, even though in the Apostle's
teaching it has become an image of marriage (cf.
Eph 5:23–33), also has value as a model of total
self-giving to God in celibacy "for the kingdom
of heaven", *in virginity consecrated to God* (cf.
Mt 19:11–12; 2 Cor 11:2). Precisely such virginity,
after the example of the Virgin of Nazareth, is the
source of a special spiritual fruitfulness: *it is the
source of motherhood in the Holy Spirit*.

But *the Church* also preserves the Faith *received
from* Christ. Following the example of Mary, who

[125] Ibid., 64.

kept and pondered in her heart everything relating to her divine Son (cf. Lk 2:19, 51), the Church is committed to preserving the word of God and investigating its riches with discernment and prudence, in order to bear faithful witness to it before all mankind in every age.[126]

44. Given Mary's relationship to the Church as an exemplar, the Church is close to her and seeks to become like her: "Imitating the Mother of her Lord, and by the power of the Holy Spirit, she preserves with virginal purity an integral faith, a firm hope, and a sincere charity."[127] Mary is thus present in the mystery of the Church as a *model*. But the Church's mystery also consists in generating people to a new and immortal life: this is her motherhood in the Holy Spirit. And here Mary is not only the model and figure of the Church; she is much more. for, *"with maternal love she cooperates in the birth and development"* of the sons and daughters of Mother Church. The Church's motherhood is accomplished not only according to the model and figure of the Mother of God but also with her "cooperation". The Church *draws* abundantly from this cooperation, that is to say from the maternal mediation which is

[126] Cf. *Dei Verbum*, 8; Saint Bonaventure, *Comment. in Evang. Lucae*, Ad Claras Aquas, VII, 53, no. 40; 68, no. 109.
[127] *Lumen Gentium*, 64.

characteristic of Mary, insofar as already on earth she cooperated in the rebirth and development of the Church's sons and daughters, as the Mother of that Son whom the Father "placed as the first-born among many brethren".[128]

She cooperated, as the Second Vatican Council teaches, with a maternal love.[129] Here we perceive the real value of the words spoken by Jesus to his Mother at the hour of the Cross: "Woman, behold your son" and to the disciple: "Behold your mother" (Jn 19:26–27). They are words which determine *Mary's place in the life of Christ's disciples* and they express—as I have already said—the new motherhood of Mother of the Redeemer: a spiritual motherhood, born from the heart of the Paschal Mystery of the Redeemer of the world. It is a motherhood in the order of grace, for it implores the gift of the Spirit who raises up the new children of God, redeemed through the sacrifice of Christ: that Spirit whom together with the Church Mary too received on the day of Pentecost.

Her motherhood is particularly noted and experienced by the Christian people at the *Sacred Banquet*—the liturgical celebration of the mystery of the Redemption—at which Christ, his *true body born of the Virgin Mary*, becomes present.

[128] Ibid., 63.
[129] Cf. ibid., 63.

The piety of the Christian people has always very rightly sensed a *profound link* between devotion to the Blessed Virgin and worship of the Eucharist: this is a fact that can be seen in the liturgy of both the West and the East, in the traditions of the Religious Families, in the modern movements of spirituality, including those for youth, and in the pastoral practice of the Marian Shrines. *Mary guides the faithful to the Eucharist.*

45. Of the essence of motherhood is the fact that it concerns the person. Motherhood always establishes *a unique and unrepeatable relationship* between two people: *between mother and child* and *between child and mother.* Even when the same woman is the mother of many children, her personal relationship with each one of them is of the very essence of motherhood. For each child is generated in a unique and unrepeatable way, and this is true both for the mother and for the child. Each child is surrounded in the same way by that maternal love on which are based the child's development and coming to maturity as a human being.

It can be said that motherhood "in the order of grace" preserves the analogy with what "in the order of nature" characterizes the union between mother and child. In the light of this fact it becomes easier to understand why in Christ's testament on Golgotha his Mother's new motherhood is expressed in the singular, in reference to one man: "Behold your son."

It can also be said that these same words fully show the reason *for the Marian dimension of the life of Christ's disciples*. This is true not only of John, who at that hour stood at the foot of the Cross together with his Master's Mother, but it is also true of every disciple of Christ, of every Christian. The Redeemer entrusts his Mother to the disciple, and at the same time he gives her to him as his Mother. Mary's motherhood which becomes man's inheritance is a gift: *a gift which Christ himself makes* personally to every individual. The Redeemer entrusts Mary to John because he entrusts John to Mary. At the foot of the Cross there begins that special *entrusting of humanity to the Mother of Christ*, which in the history of the Church has been practiced and expressed in different ways. The same Apostle and Evangelist, after reporting the words addressed by Jesus on the Cross to his Mother and to himself, adds: "And from that hour the disciple took her to his own home" (Jn 19:27). This statement certainly means that the role of son was attributed to the disciple and that he assumed responsibility for the Mother of his beloved Master. And since Mary was given as a mother to him personally, the statement indicates, even though indirectly, everything expressed by the intimate relationship of a child with its mother. And all of this can be included in the word "entrusting". Such entrusting is *the response* to a person's love, and in particular *to the love of a mother*.

The Marian dimension of the life of a disciple of Christ is expressed in a special way precisely through this filial entrusting to the Mother of Christ, which began with the testament of the Redeemer on Golgotha. Entrusting himself to Mary in a filial manner, the Christian, like the Apostle John, "welcomes" the Mother of Christ "into his own home"[130] and brings her into everything that makes up his inner life, that is to say into his human and Christian "I": he *"took her to his own home"*. Thus the Christian seeks to be taken into that "maternal charity" with which the Redeemer's Mother "cares for the brethren of her Son",[131] "in whose birth and development she cooperates"[132] in the measure of the gift proper to each one through the power of Christ's Spirit. Thus also is

---

[130] Clearly, in the Greek text the expression "εἰς τὰ ἴδια" goes beyond the mere acceptance of Mary by the disciple in the sense of material lodging and hospitality in his house; it indicates rather a *communion of life* established between the two as a result of the words of the dying *Christ*: cf. Saint Augustine, *In Ioan. Evang. tract.* 119, 3: *CCL* 36, 659: "He took her to himself, not into his own property, for he possessed nothing of his own, but among his own duties, which he attended to with dedication."

[131] *Lumen Gentium*, 62.

[132] Ibid., 63.

exercised that motherhood in the Spirit which became Mary's role at the foot of the Cross and in the Upper Room.

46. This filial relationship, this self-entrusting of a child to its mother, not only has its *beginning in Christ* but can also be said to be *definitively directed toward him*. Mary can be said to continue to say to each individual the words which she spoke at Cana in Galilee: "Do whatever he tells you." For he, Christ, is the one Mediator between God and mankind; he is "the way, and the truth, and the life" (Jn 14:6); it is he whom the Father has given to the world, so that man "should not perish but have eternal life" (Jn 3:16). The Virgin of Nazareth became the first "witness" of this saving love of the Father and she also wishes *to remain* its *humble handmaid always and everywhere*. For every Christian, for every human being, Mary is the one who first "believed", and precisely with her faith as Spouse and Mother she wishes to act upon all those who entrust themselves to her as her children. And it is well known that the more her children persevere and progress in this attitude, the nearer Mary leads them to the "unsearchable riches of Christ" (Eph 3:8). And to the same degree they recognize more and more clearly the dignity of man in all its fullness and the definitive meaning of his voca-

tion, for "Christ . . . fully reveals man to man himself."[133]

This Marian dimension of Christian life takes on special importance in relation to women and their status. In fact, femininity has a *unique relationship* with the Mother of the Redeemer, a subject which can be studied in greater depth elsewhere. Here I simply wish to note that the figure of Mary of Nazareth sheds light on *womanhood as such* by the very fact that God, in the sublime event of the Incarnation of his Son, entrusted himself to the ministry, the free and active ministry of a woman. It can thus be said that women, by looking to Mary, find in her the secret of living their femininity with dignity and of achieving their own true advancement. In the light of Mary, the Church sees in the face of women the reflection of a beauty which mirrors the loftiest sentiments of which the human heart is capable: the self-offering totality of love; the strength that is capable of bearing the greatest sorrows; limitless fidelity and tireless devotion to work; the ability to combine penetrating intuition with words of support and encouragement.

47. At the Council Paul VI solemnly proclaimed that *Mary is the Mother of the Church*, "that is,

[133] *Gaudium et Spes*, 22.

Mother of the entire Christian people, both faithful and pastors".[134] Later, in 1968, in the Profession of Faith known as the "Credo of the People of God", he restated this truth in an even more forceful way in these words: "We believe that the Most Holy Mother of God, the new Eve, the Mother of the Church, carries on in heaven her maternal role with regard to the members of Christ, cooperating in the birth and development of divine life in the souls of the redeemed."[135]

The Council's teaching emphasized that the truth concerning the Blessed Virgin, Mother of Christ, is an effective aid in exploring more deeply the truth concerning the Church. When speaking of the Constitution *Lumen Gentium* which had just been approved by the Council, Paul VI said: "Knowledge of the true Catholic doctrine regarding the Blessed Virgin Mary will always be a key to *the exact understanding of the mystery of Christ and of the Church*."[136] Mary is present *in* the Church as the Mother of Christ, and at the same time as that Mother whom Christ, in the mystery of

[134] Cf. Pope Paul VI, *Discourse of November 21, 1964: AAS* 56 (1964) 1015.

[135] Pope Paul VI, *Solemn Profession of Faith* (June 30, 1968), 15: *AAS* 60 (1968) 438f.

[136] Pope Paul VI, *Discourse of November 21, 1964: AAS* 56 (1964) 1015.

the Redemption, gave to humanity in the person of the Apostle John. Thus, in her new motherhood in the Spirit, Mary embraces each and every one *in* the Church, and embraces each and every one *through* the Church. In this sense Mary, Mother of the Church, is also the Church's model. Indeed, as Paul VI hopes and asks, the Church must draw "from the Virgin Mother of God the most authentic form of perfect imitation of Christ".[137]

Thanks to this special bond linking the Mother of Christ with the Church, there is further *clarified the mystery of that "woman"* who, from the first chapters of the Book of Genesis until the Book of Revelation, accompanies the revelation of God's salvific plan for humanity. For Mary, present in the Church as the Mother of the Redeemer, takes part, as a mother, in that "monumental struggle against the powers of darkness"[138] which continues throughout human history. And by her ecclesial identification as the "woman clothed with the sun" (Rev 12:1),[139] it can be said that "in the Most Holy Virgin the Church has already reached that perfection whereby she exists with-

[137] Ibid., 1016.

[138] Cf. *Gaudium et Spes*, 37.

[139] Cf. Saint Bernard, *In Dominica infra oct. Assumptionis Sermo*: *S. Bernardi Opera*, V, 1968, 262–74.

out spot or wrinkle". Hence, as Christians raise their eyes with faith to Mary in the course of their earthly pilgrimage, they "strive to increase in holiness".[140] Mary, the exalted Daughter of Zion, helps all her children, wherever they may be and whatever their condition, *to find in Christ the path to the Father's house*.

Thus the Church, throughout her life, maintains with the Mother of God a link which embraces, in the saving mystery, the past, the present, and the future, and venerates her as the spiritual Mother of humanity and the advocate of grace.

3. *The meaning of the Marian Year*

48. It is precisely the special bond between humanity and this Mother which has led me to proclaim a Marian Year in the Church, in this period before the end of the Second Millennium since Christ's birth. A similar initiative was taken in the past, when Pius XII proclaimed 1954 as a Marian Year, in order to highlight the exceptional holiness of the Mother of Christ as expressed in the mysteries of her Immaculate Conception (defined exactly a century before) and of her Assumption into heaven.[141]

[140] *Lumen Gentium*, 65.
[141] Cf. Encyclical Letter *Fulgens Corona* (September 8, 1953): *AAS* 45 (1953) 577–92. Pius X with his Encyclical

Now, following the line of the Second Vatican Council, I wish to emphasize the *special presence* of the Mother of God in the mystery of Christ and his Church. For this is a fundamental dimension emerging from the Mariology of the Council, the end of which is now more than twenty years behind us. The Extraordinary Synod of Bishops held in 1985 exhorted everyone to follow faithfully the teaching and guidelines of the Council. We can say that these two events—the Council and the Synod—embody what the Holy Spirit himself wishes "to say to the Church" in the present phase of history.

In this context, the Marian Year is meant to promote a new and more careful reading of what the Council said about the Blessed Virgin Mary, Mother of God, in the mystery of Christ and of the Church, the topic to which the contents of this Encyclical are devoted. Here we speak not only of *the doctrine of faith* but also of *the life of faith*, and thus of authentic "Marian spirituality", seen in the light of Tradition, and especially the spirituality to which the Council exhorts us.[142] Furthermore,

Letter *Ad Diem Illum* (February 2, 1904), on the occasion of the 50th anniversary of the dogmatic definition of the Immaculate Conception of the Blessed Virgin Mary, had proclaimed an Extraordinary Jubilee of a few months; *Pii X P.M. Acta*, I, 147–66.

[142] Cf. *Lumen Gentium*, 66–67.

Marian *spirituality*, like its corresponding *devotion*, finds a very rich source in the historical experience of individuals and of the various Christian communities present among the different peoples and nations of the world. In this regard, I would like to recall, among the many witnesses and teachers of this spirituality, the figure of Saint Louis Marie Grignion de Montfort,[143] who proposes consecration to Christ through the hands of Mary, as an effective means for Christians to live faithfully their baptismal commitments. I am pleased to note that in our own time too new manifestations of this spirituality and devotion are not lacking.

There thus exist solid points of reference to look to and follow in the context of this Marian Year.

49. This Marian Year *will begin on the Solemnity of Pentecost*, on the seventh of June next (June 7, 1987). For it is a question not only of recalling that Mary "preceded" the entry of Christ the Lord into the history of the human family, but also of emphasizing, in the light of Mary, that from the moment when the mystery of the Incarnation was accom-

[143] Saint Louis Marie Grignion de Montfort, *Traité de la vraie dévotion à la sainte Vierge* [Treatise on the True Devotion to the Holy Virgin] This saint can rightly be linked with the figure of Saint Alfonsus Maria de Liguori, the second centenary of whose death occurs this year; cf., among his works, *The Glories of Mary*.

plished human history entered "the fullness of time", and that the Church is the sign of this fullness. As the People of God, the Church makes her pilgrim way toward eternity through faith, in the midst of all the peoples and nations, beginning from the day of Pentecost. *Christ's Mother*, who was present at the beginning of "the time of the Church", when in expectation of the coming of the Holy Spirit she devoted herself to prayer in the midst of the Apostles and her Son's disciples, constantly "precedes" *the Church* in her *journey* through human history. She is also the one who, precisely as the "handmaid of the Lord", cooperates unceasingly with the work of salvation accomplished by Christ, her Son.

Thus by means of this Marian Year *the Church is called* not only to remember everything in her past that testifies to the special maternal cooperation of the Mother of God in the work of salvation in Christ the Lord, but also, on her own part, *to prepare* for the future the paths of this cooperation. For the end of the Second Christian Millennium opens up as a new prospect.

50. As has already been mentioned, also among our divided brethren many honor and celebrate the Mother of the Lord, especially among the Orientals. It is a Marian light cast upon ecumenism. In particular, I wish to mention once more that

during the Marian Year there will occur the *Millennium of the Baptism* of Saint Vladimir, Grand Duke of Kiev (988). This marked the beginning of Christianity in the territories of what was then called Rus', and subsequently in other territories of Eastern Europe. In this way, through the work of evangelization, Christianity spread beyond Europe, as far as the northern territories of the Asian continent. We would therefore like, especially during this Year, to join in prayer with all those who are celebrating the Millennium of this Baptism, both Orthodox and Catholics, repeating and confirming with the Council those sentiments of joy and comfort that "the Easterners . . . with ardent emotion and devout mind concur in reverencing the Mother of God, ever Virgin".[144] Even though we are still experiencing the painful effects of the separation which took place some decades later (1054), we can say that *in the presence of the Mother of Christ we feel that we are true brothers and sisters* within that messianic People, which is called to be the one family of God on earth. As I announced at the beginning of the New Year: "We desire to reconfirm this universal inheritance of all the sons and daughters of this earth."[145]

In announcing the Year of Mary, I also indicated

[144] *Lumen Gentium*, 69.
[145] Homily on January 1, 1987.

that it will end next year on *the Solemnity of the Assumption of the Blessed Virgin into Heaven*, in order to emphasize the "great sign in heaven" spoken of by the *Apocalypse*. In this way we also wish to respond to the exhortation of the Council, which looks to Mary as "a sign of sure hope and solace for the pilgrim People of God". And the Council expresses this exhortation in the following words: "Let the entire body of the faithful pour forth persevering prayer to the Mother of God and Mother of mankind. Let them implore that she who aided the beginning of the Church by her prayers may now, exalted as she is in heaven above all the saints and angels, intercede with her Son in the fellowship of all the saints. May she do so until all the peoples of the human family, whether they are honored with the name of Christian or whether they still do not know their Savior, are happily gathered together in peace and harmony into the one People of God, for the glory of the Most Holy and Undivided Trinity."[146]

[146] *Lumen Gentium*, 69.

CONCLUSION

51. At the end of the daily Liturgy of the Hours, among the invocations addressed to Mary by the Church is the following:

"Loving Mother of the Redeemer,
Gate of Heaven, Star of the Sea,
Assist your people who have fallen yet strive to
   rise again.
To the wonderment of nature your bore your
   Creator!"

"To the wonderment of nature!" These words of the antiphon express that *wonderment of faith* which accompanies the mystery of Mary's divine motherhood. In a sense, it does so in the heart of the whole of creation, and, directly, in the heart of the whole People of God, in the heart of the Church. How wonderfully far God has gone, the Creator and Lord of all things, in the "revelation of himself" to man![147] How clearly he has bridged all the

[147] Cf. *Dei Verbum*, 2: "Through this revelation . . . the invisible God . . . out of the abundance of his love speaks to

spaces of that infinite "distance" which separates the Creator from the creature! If in himself he remains *ineffable and unsearchable*, still more *ineffable and unsearchable is he in the reality of the Incarnation* of the Word, who became man through the Virgin of Nazareth.

If he has eternally willed to call man to share in the divine nature (cf. 2 Pet 1:4), it can be said that he has matched the "divinization" of man to humanity's historical conditions, so that even after sin he is ready to restore at a great price the eternal plan of his love through the "humanization" of his Son, who is of the same being as himself. The whole of creation, and more directly man himself, cannot fail to be amazed at this gift in which he has become a sharer, in the Holy Spirit: "God so loved the world that he gave his only Son" (Jn 3:16).

At the center of this mystery, in the midst of this wonderment of faith, stands Mary. As the loving Mother of the Redeemer, she was the first to experience it: "To the wonderment of nature you bore your Creator!"

52. The words of this liturgical antiphon also express *the truth of the "great transformation"* which the mystery of the Incarnation establishes for man.

---

men as friends . . . and lives among them . . . so that he may invite and take them into fellowship with himself."

It is a transformation which belongs to his entire history, from that beginning which is revealed to us in the first chapters of Genesis until the final end, in the perspective of the end of the world, of which Jesus has revealed to us "neither the day nor the hour" (Mt 25:13). It is an unending and continuous transformation between falling and rising again, between the man of sin and the man of grace and justice. The Advent liturgy in particular is at the very heart of this transformation and captures its unceasing "here and now" when it exclaims: "Assist your people who have fallen yet strive to rise again!"

These words apply to every individual, every community, to nations and peoples, and to the generations and epochs of human history, to our own epoch, to these years the Millennium which is drawing to a close: "Assist, yes assist, your people who have fallen!"

This is the invocation addressed to Mary, the "loving Mother of the Redeemer", the invocation addressed to Christ, who through Mary entered human history. Year after year the antiphon rises to Mary, evoking that moment which saw the accomplishment of this essential historical transformation, which irreversibly continues: the transformation from "falling" to "rising".

Mankind has made wonderful discoveries and achieved extraordinary results in the fields of science and technology. It has made great advances along the path of progress and civilization, and in recent times one could say that it has succeeded in speeding up the pace of history. But the fundamental trans-formation, the one which can be called "original", constantly accompanies man's journey, and through all the events of history accompanies each and every individual. It is the transformation from "falling" to "rising", from death to life. It is also *a constant challenge* to people's consciences, a challenge to man's whole historical awareness: the challenge to follow the path of "not falling" in ways that are ever old and ever new, and of "rising again" if a fall has occurred.

As she goes forward with the whole of humanity toward the frontier between the two Millennia, the Church, for her part, with the whole com-munity of believers and in union with all men and women of good will, takes up the great challenge contained in these words of the Marian antiphon: "the people who have fallen yet strive to rise again", and she addresses both the Redeemer and his Mother with the plea: "Assist us." For, as this prayer attests, the Church sees the Blessed Mother of God in the saving mystery of Christ and in her own mystery. She sees Mary deeply rooted in humanity's history, in man's eternal vocation according to the providential plan which God has made for him from eternity. She sees Mary maternally present and sharing in the many complicated problems which *today* beset the lives of individuals, families, and nations; she sees her helping the Christian people in the constant struggle between good and evil, to ensure that it "does not fall", or, if it has fallen, that it "rises again".

I hope with all my heart that the reflections contained in the present Encyclical will also serve to renew this vision in the hearts of all believers.

As Bishop of Rome, I send to all those to whom these thoughts are addressed the kiss of peace, my greeting, and my blessing in our Lord Jesus Christ. Amen.

Given in Rome, at Saint Peter's, on March 25, the Solemnity of the Annunciation of the Lord, in the year 1987, the ninth of my Pontificate.

JOHN PAUL II

Commentary

by

HANS URS VON BALTHASAR

the light of Mary, the Church sees in the face of women the reflection of a beauty that mirrors the loftiest sentiments of which the human heart is capable: the self-offering totality of love; the strength that is capable of bearing the greatest sorrows; limitless fidelity and tireless devotion to work; the ability to combine penetrating intuition with words of comfort and encouragement" (*RM*, no. 46).

Mary represents all this, we may add in closing, with such inscrutable feminine simplicity as is quite unattainable for a man in his "busy-ness". The encyclical touches "with wonderment" on the mystery that is Mary, and displays before our eyes many resulting reflections. And yet, after all, it simply desires to show Mary's unassuming, undivided "fullness of grace", a grace deriving entirely from the "overflowing richness of Christ" and comprehensible only from there. And though we may satisfy the exegetes by acknowledging the Magnificat as representing, not Mary's thoughts, but the Evangelist's formulations, in the end we still possess those two plainest of plain utterances that are enough to reveal the unfathomable simplicity of her heart: "I am the handmaid of the Lord", and "Do whatever he tells you".

Preface

Our Holy Father's encyclical on the occasion of the Marian Year is highly significant in several respects. Its fluent style, on the surface, makes for easy reading and understanding. Yet its conception flows from a vision of Mary's mystery so profound and essential that the reader's decisive effort is required in order to discover the encyclical's central focus and not to see only the multiple lines of reflection emanating from it.

We approach the encyclical first with an observation regarding its general composition. It presents a thoroughly original synthesis between the closing chapter on Mary of the Council's great document, *Lumen Gentium*, and the Holy Father's most personal insights into his topic: Mary and the Church. The Council had used extremely cautious and nonemphatic language in formulating the basic teaching that Mary is model and "type" for the

This commentary on *Redemptoris Mater* was translated from German by Rev. Lothar Krauth.

Church. As a rough initial assessment, we may state that the encyclical goes a few steps further than that, not less cautiously, however, and always mindful of ecumenical implications.

These further steps are not taken tentatively or without clear direction, but firmly and decisively, springing from a deeper reflection on the Council's teaching. We shall show how this expansion of a typically "Catholic" topic (as is assumed in many quarters) unexpectedly opens new possibilities in view of Western ecumenism. Here, the longstanding ecumenical rule is vindicated once again: each denomination should first explore the depths of its own beliefs rather than try to reach out, for these depths may indeed provide the common ground to meet the other.

The structure

A first glance over all three parts of the encyclical will provide but a hint of the strict logic governing the construction and elaboration of the topic.

Chapter 1, "Mary in the Mystery of Christ", states clearly that all Mariology finds its proper place within the context of Christology; it is justified and comprehended only from there (*RM*, no. 4). This is explained by using the well-known opening of the Letter to the Ephesians, which outlines God's comprehensive plan of salvation, conceived "before all creation". The privileged role of the Blessed Mother can thus be identified: God the Father "chose us before the world began; he predestined us, in love, to be his adopted sons through Christ Jesus, that all might praise the glorious favor he has bestowed on us through the blood of his beloved Son, in whom we have forgiveness of sins" (see Eph 1:4–7). If this is so, then inevitably the question arises, How, indeed, could this beloved Son become man in order to shed his blood on the Cross for our sins? As Saint Paul puts it, he had to be "born of woman". This woman, to bear him fittingly and according to God's will, could not be sinful and therefore disobedient. Even though being a part of humanity receiving redemption, she would have to be preredeemed; for she would be the Mother of the Redeemer, and as such be one of the conditions for his potential Incarnation. This privilege would remain with her permanently, as brought out in the second part of the encyclical.

Chapter 2 is titled "The Mother of God at the Center of the Pilgrim Church". Mary is certainly an integrated member of the Church, yet she does not lose her identity as Mother of the Redeemer or as model, because of her pre-redemption, for authentic life and attitude in the Church. The full reality of the Church derives from the Cross, the Resurrection, and the outpouring of the Holy

Spirit. But this means that prior to the birth of the Church, we have to acknowledge her Founder, and not only him but his mother as well, who was overshadowed by the Holy Spirit and thus, as it were, experienced an anticipated Pentecost. Jesus on the Cross implied this consideration when he entrusted Mary to his disciple John, one of the Apostles, and so incorporated her unique and permanent motherhood into his nascent Church. For this reason, Pope Paul VI formally conferred on her the title "Mother of the Church".

Chapter 3, "Maternal Mediation", is based on the premises just stated. The virgin of Nazareth was chosen to be the Mother of the Redeemer. This is such a singular event that her mediating role necessarily now extends throughout the history of the Church, even of the world—since Jesus did not just redeem the Church but the world. Seen in this light, the controversial term "Mediatrix" (*Lumen Gentium*, no. 62) loses much of its difficulty.

This preliminary synthesis still remains entirely on the surface; the all-embracing unifying concept lies deeper, more hidden. In the following considerations we shall try to identify the foundational pillars of the encyclical by distinguishing three central lines of thought: Mary's faith, Mary as "preceding" Christ's founding of the Church, and Mary as virgin and mother. But these groups of thought must not be taken separately or simply in relation to each other; we have to try to discover them as emanating from one and the same central concept: Mary is totally free from guile, "simple" in the sense of the gospel, the perfect example of the Beatitudes' "poor in spirit". For this reason, all our various attempts to approach her marvelously simple mystery can succeed only if we are able to trace all our lines of reflection, however enlightening, back to that one luminous aura of grace that surrounds the simple handmaid of the Lord, "the woman clothed with the sun".

Faith

Through ingenious inspiration, the encyclical gives a most prominent place to Mary's faith. Perhaps never before in Mariology has this been done with such decisiveness. Thus the Mother of the Lord is given a place that clearly points back to Abraham, the ancestor of God's covenant with humanity, but equally points ahead to the "pilgrim journey of the Church". "Blest is she who trusted that the Lord's words to her would be fulfilled" (Lk 1:45). These words spoken by Elizabeth (*RM*, no. 12) are like "a key that unlocks for us the innermost reality of Mary" (*RM*, no. 19). At the Annunciation Mary, by her faith, already "entrusted herself to God completely, with the full submission of intellect and will, manifesting the obedience of faith to him who spoke to her through his messenger" (*RM*, no. 13). Thus, as in Saint Augustine's famous expression, Mary "conceived in her spirit before she conceived in her womb". Obedience to God in faith involves a person more intimately than mere knowledge does.

Mary is given the prophecy about a child she is to bear, who will not be begotten by a man and who is destined to occupy the throne of his father David, even to be called "Son of the Most High". At this point, the Pope asks a question without providing the answer: Could Mary grasp, "at the moment of the Annunciation, the vital significance of the angel's words? And how is one to understand that 'kingdom' which will have no end?" (*RM*, no. 15). Much less could she grasp the full meaning—though she "kept and pondered everything in her heart"—when she receives the prophecy that designated her child to be "a sign which will be opposed"; when she hears the prediction that her soul would be "pierced with a sword" (Lk 2:34; *RM*, no. 16); and when she is puzzled by the remark of her twelve-year-old boy (*RM*, no. 17). She can foresee suffering, even soon experience it (on the flight to Egypt), yet as mother she "is in contact with the truth about her Son only in faith and through faith" (*RM*, no. 17). And even though the angel predicted her child would be "Son of the Most High", she, his mother, "lived in intimacy with this mystery only through faith" (*RM*, no. 17). This mystery is completed at the Cross where this Son, prophesied to be "great" and "sitting on the throne of David", comes to an agonizing end as one rejected by all the world. Here, through faith, "Mary is perfectly united with Christ in his deepest self-humiliation (*kenosis*)", and "this is perhaps the deepest *kenosis* of faith in human history" (*RM*, no. 18). At the foot of the Cross, the words "Blessed is she who believed" attain their most profound meaning (*RM*, no. 19).

Here, Mary's faith completes the faith of Abraham who did not falter even when faced with utter contradiction, with the order to sacrifice Isaac, the son of the promise (*RM*, no. 26). In her "Magnificat", Mary directly refers to Abraham (*RM*, no. 36), and thus shows that she considers herself the completion of the Old Covenant. But the Church Fathers (especially Irenaeus) rightly trace her obedience in faith even further back, to our first parents: "The knot of Eve's disobedience was untied by Mary's obedience" (*RM*, no. 19). We mentioned already that this primordial faith of Mary was an essential part of God's design before all time. Just as, in the first book of the Bible, we find the "woman", whose offspring will crush the serpent's head, so do we find her again at the center of the last book, as the "woman clothed with the sun", bringing forth the Messiah (*RM*, nos. 11, 24, 52). Mary's faith spans the whole of salvation history; consequently, her role in this history can be understood "in faith only" (*RM*, no. 38). Faith as lived by Mary is total, trusting self-surrender of mind and body to God; it is absence of understanding; it is uncalculating obedience; it is self-effacing, living humility; but it is also acceptance of responsibility to do God's bidding.

It is obvious that the encyclical, given its ecumenical intent, dedicates ample space to the Marian devotion of the Christian Orient. Six entire sections (nos. 29–34 and 50) speak about it: there exists "an authentic pilgrimage of faith in space and time, during which Eastern Christians have always looked with boundless trust to the Mother of the Lord, celebrated her with praise, and invoked her with unceasing prayer" (no. 31). Not much is said about the separated churches of the West, even though they, too, are invited to "deepen . . . that obedience of faith of which Mary is the first and brightest example" (no. 29). But does not the encyclical, insisting as it does on the priority of Mary's faith, in truth engage in an undeclared, passionate dialogue with Martin Luther? We have only to consult his beautiful commentary on the "Magnificat". Do we not find there—certain polemical passages notwithstanding—an astonishing counterpart to the Pope's commentary? (nos. 35f.).

Luther, too, emphasizes that Mary's faith was sheer, humble self-surrender to God's grace ("true humility means not to be aware of being humble"). And then: "You see that David, Saint Peter, Saint Paul, Saint Mary Magdalen, and others like them— by the exceeding grace undeservedly bestowed on them for the edification of all people—have become examples to build up our confidence and faith. Do you not think that the Blessed Mother of God as well would willingly and readily be such an example for all the world?" After having discussed Abraham and his "seed", Christ, and the unity of the Old with the New Covenant, Luther concludes with a prayer to God "for a true understanding" of the Magnificat, so that it may "not merely shine and talk, but burn and live in body and soul. This grant us Christ through the intercession and intention of his dear mother Mary! Amen." (Later, to be sure, Luther repudiated the notion of intercession.)

Since we thus agree on the Mother of the Lord as the unique model of Christian faith, "Why", the Pope asks, "should we not all together look to her as our common Mother, who prays for the unity of God's family, and who 'precedes' us all at the head of the long line of witnesses of the Faith in the one Lord?" (*RM*, no. 30).

Considerations on the model character of Mary's faith lead us directly to a second basic concept of the encyclical.

Mary the "Prototype"

Mary's living faith, from the Annunciation to the Cross, precedes in time the actual "founding" of the Church on the Cross, on Easter, and on Pentecost. And not only in time, but also in a spiritual sense, for Mary's living faith is the perfect prototype of what is expected in the life of the Church; a prototype, however, whose perfection the Church will never be able to equal until the end of time.

The encyclical repeatedly states this relationship in ever new terms by pointing out the parallel elements between Mary's being overshadowed by the Holy Spirit and the descent of that same Spirit on the disciples on Pentecost, in whose midst Mary is found praying. It then emphasizes the "unique correspondence between the moment of the Incarnation of the Word and the moment of the birth of the Church. The person who links these two moments is Mary", but her humble, unassuming presence points away from herself and to the "birth from the Holy Spirit" (*RM*, no. 24). "The moment of Pentecost in Jerusalem had been prepared for by the moment of the Annunciation in Nazareth, as well as by the Cross" (*RM*, no. 26; cf. nos. 40, 44). (Incidentally, this makes us appreciate the decision to begin the Marian Year with Pentecost 1987; cf. *RM*, no. 49).

The decisive aspect of this correlation consists in the fact that Mary's entire journey of faith—up to the Cross and the Resurrection, which changed the dark night of her faith into bright certitude—constantly "precedes" the Church's journey through history (*RM*, no. 49). Mary's "heroic faith . . . precedes the apostolic witness of the Church", a witness that begins with the missionary preaching on Pentecost. The Apostles and all those who follow in their footsteps receive into their witness a portion of Mary's preceding witness, and thus "in a sense share in Mary's faith". The Magnificat brings it out: all generations will praise her faith and so "seek in her faith support for their own faith" (*RM*, no. 27). "Mary's faith, embedded in the Church's apostolic witness, continues to become the faith of the pilgrim People of God, the faith of individuals and communities in the Church" (*RM*, no. 28). This is so because Mary's faith, the culmination of Israel's entire journey of faith, has entered into "the very heart" of Christ's fullness (*RM*, no. 36). Only as the fullness of faith, as the unconditional Yes, was her faith fit to become one of the conditions for the Incarnation of God's Word.

This insight allows the Pope to take a deliberate step beyond the Mariology of the Council as found in the decree *Lumen Gentium*. He wholeheartedly reconfirms the teaching on Mary as the "permanent model", the "example", the "type" for the Church's faith (*RM*, no. 42). But the Church is rightly seen as bringing forth, in the mystery of the sacraments, new spiritual life. And if the Church can thus claim motherhood in the Holy Spirit, then "Mary is not only the model and type of the Church; she is much more" (*RM*, no. 44). Saint Augustine states it repeatedly in most of his writings: Mary brings forth the head; the Church brings forth the members, the body. Mary herself, then, through her own everlasting motherhood "cooperates in the birth and development of the sons and daughters of Mother Church" (*RM*, no. 44). Mary's link to her Son was a unique person–to–person relationship. In the same way, her maternal relation to every Christian constitutes an "unrepeatable relationship between two people: between mother and child, and between child and mother. . . . For each child is generated in a unique and unrepeatable way, and this is true both for the mother and for the child" (*RM*, no. 45).

Here, now, the "prototype" of Mary's motherhood implies various consequences for the Church and every Christian. First, Mary's abundantly effective faith, especially under the Cross, is, by her dying Son, made part of his actions in bringing forth the Church. This justifies the title "Mother of the Church", bestowed on Mary by Pope Paul VI (*RM*, no. 47). Then, we have to realize that Mary's entire life experience with her Son, her whole faith-memory, is handed on to the Church; not only insofar as some of these memories have explicitly become part of the infancy narratives in the Gospel, but even more so because all her salvific responses, preceding Christ's redemption proper, have been spiritually incorporated into the Faith of the Church, so that now "the Church draws abundantly" from this treasure (*RM*, no. 44). Finally, Mary's timeless creative and generative cooperation in the baptismal birth and Christian development of each Christian, as mentioned above, effects a personal relationship between each Christian's faith and Mary's motherhood. For this motherhood is by no means exclusively spiritual, though we usually tend to think of the Church's motherhood as being such. Mary's motherhood is immensely real, tangible, a matter of factual experience; after all, her child was the historical Jesus Christ whose life, death, and Resurrection have gained us salvation. We celebrate Mary's Assumption into heaven, not to remove her from us beyond our reach, not to turn her into a mere spiritual ideal, but rather to remind ourselves that we are close to her in a very real, even physical relationship.

The third and final basic concept of the encyclical points in this direction.

"The fruit of thy womb"

This Marian encyclical does not construct a complete Mariological system but simply presents some highlights; it is up to the faithful reader to go from there with further reflections.

One of the main concepts, as we have seen, was this: Mary, through her perfect faith "in her spirit", becomes the Redeemer's mother "in her body"; and this bodily aspect is part of the reality of the Church's motherhood as well. True, during his life on earth Jesus saw fit to de-emphasize all mere blood-relationships (Lk 8:20f.; 11:27f.), in order to counter misunderstandings and to show that in his Church "motherhood and brotherhood" would be based on faith. (Yet Mary, too, was the model precisely for this! Cf. *RM*, no. 20: "Through faith Mary continued to hear the word and keep it", that word "which surpasses all understanding".) But this does not at all mean that the Church, the "Body of Christ", and "born from his wounded side", would be a purely spiritual reality.

The Pope considers the specific place of Mary with regard to the call of the Apostles during Christ's public life (*RM*, no. 26); he especially considers the link, established from the Cross, between Mary and the Apostle John who becomes her "son", and through whom she is incorporated into the visible Church community because John "symbolizes the Church" (*RM*, no. 24). And when we hear that John "took her to his own home" we understand it as the forming of a living bond between the two, in response to the word of the dying Christ (*RM*, no. 45). Thus, at the Cross, the inward personal sanctity (Mary) and the outward, visible authority of the Church (the Apostles) are being linked, one to the other.

The question of Mary's marriage to Joseph (whose fruitful virginity expresses the completion of the Old Covenant since Abraham and Sarah) and the question of Mary's union with John (a virginal primordial cell of the Church-to-be) are not discussed in the encyclical. Both topics, however, would indicate to what extent Mary's role touches even on the area of human sexual relationships. Her virginity, in the sense of unreserved openness to God, is seen, indeed, as having no other justification than this: that she may become the physical mother of God's Word in the flesh. A realism based on the reality of human existence in the body is evident in one particular section of the encyclical, where it speaks of "a renewed commitment" of the Church "near the end of the second Christian Millennium". In the Magnificat, Mary expresses her "preferential love for the poor", shows herself "deeply imbued with the spirit of the poor of Yahweh" and prophesies "the coming of the Messiah of the poor" (cf. Is 11:4; 61:1).

All this refers to God's own "preferential love for the poor and humble", and so directs the Church to adopt an "option in favor of the poor" (*RM*, no. 37). "These are matters and questions intimately connected with the Christian meaning of freedom and liberation." This "Christian meaning", then, is implied in the message of the Magnificat, which is itself no more than a synthesis of God's saving actions in the Old Covenant and which, indeed, does not make of Mary a "revolutionary rationalist". Rather, the Pope is quoting from the Instruction on Christian Freedom and Liberation, issued in 1986 by the Congregation for the Doctrine of the Faith: "Mary is totally dependent upon God and, through her faith, completely directed toward him; and, at the side of her Son, she is the most perfect image of freedom and liberation of humanity and of the universe" (*RM*, no. 37).

Mary, in her canticle of praise, has "magnified the Lord" because he "lifts up the lowly" and "fills the hungry with good things"; a praise uttered not just in some general sense but certainly also because Mary, more than any other of God's children, was personally aware of such lowliness: for God, the Almighty, "has looked on his servant in her lowliness". Mary rejoices in him who "is mighty", not because she has been "lifted up", but because God "has looked on his servant". She is indeed poor in a material sense, yet she rejoices not over any material gifts (experiences like the flight into Egypt would mean quite the opposite!) but over the gift without price, over the privilege of being mother of the Messiah. And this gift is not so much a favor to her personally, as rather the expression of God's mercy on his "servant Israel", whose yearning of old for "Abraham's seed" has finally been satisfied. In her "option for the poor", then, Mary is entirely herself; she has by no means been changed into a "different Mary".

Mary is fully aware that by God's favor, and in an unrepeatable, unparalleled manner, she has become mother, not only of her Son, but through him also of all those who in his name have become sons and daughters of the Church. (The term "Church" here does not imply any defined boundaries, for Christ's saving grace is indeed offered to all humanity before and after him.) As far as Mary is this singular mother, she relates to every child of God. Whatever the encyclical states, in several passages, about her motherly, mediating intercession—beginning in Cana (*RM*, no. 21) where she intercedes for people's needs and "speaks for her Son", up to her eternal mission in heaven —all this flows directly from her being mother. "Mary's mediation is intimately linked with her motherhood; it possesses a specifically maternal character" (*RM*, no. 38). In this, very importantly, she stands at the center of the "communion of saints" (*RM*, no. 41), she is, as it were, "clothed by the whole reality of the communion of saints" (*RM*, no. 41). Yes, it is this communion of saints that is the practical expression of our "being-for-each-other" in God's kingdom and that also shows in supernatural perfection one of the most beautiful human potentials present even on the purely natural level: to be able to care and intercede for each other, especially in times of trouble. Mary, by her being the Mother of the Messiah, from the outset occupies a place at the very center of a world in deep trouble, "at the very center of that enmity" which permeates the history of the world and of our salvation (*RM*, no. 11). She has to live her faithful obedience "in misunderstanding and sorrow" (*RM*, no. 16) and thus is gifted with motherly compassion for the misery of her children.

When Jesus, finally, addresses her simply as "woman", the strange expression reported in John's Gospel, he indicates that he, the man and Second Adam, indeed sees in her the figure of woman as such. This is the case in Cana where she offers her intercession, and at the Cross where she suffers with Jesus as no other ever has suffered with him. She lives her womanhood as virgin, as mother, as bride, and as spouse. If she is recognized as the prototype of woman, then it becomes most evident how utterly absurd it would be to imagine Mary acting as a priest, perhaps preaching or even uttering the words of consecration. "Women, by looking to Mary, find in her the secret of living their femininity with dignity, and of achieving their own true advancement. In